Special Pra████████████ ██ ██ *he Sex*

"It's Not About the Sex of.. ...pc and direction to those recovering from sexual compulsivity. As daunting as recovery can seem, this book helps readers gain a sense of calm by recognizing key issues that will move them forward in their lives. Susskind provides a pathway to let go of shame while garnering self-compassion and understanding. The author's years of experience also bring depth and breadth to the healing process. From living in fantasy to embracing reality, from letting go of perfectionism and image management to accepting the imperfections of humanity, and through its exploration of the possibilities of recovery, this powerful book reinforces the reader's commitment to sexual sobriety."

Claudia Black, PhD
Author, *Unspoken Legacy* and *Intimate Treason*

"Going beyond current tension around out-of-control sexual behaviors, such as whether we should link sexual compulsivity to a pathologizing, disease-oriented addiction model, Susskind addresses the need for humans to learn how to connect, love, and thrive in intimate relationships. The author cites brokenheartedness as cause, and his is a fresh, much needed voice in the barren landscape of treating and overcoming problematic sexual expression. This is an openhearted framework for navigating toward a life filled with healthy sexual pleasures."

Patti Britton, PhD, MPH
Clinical Sexologist, Sex Coach, and Cofounder of SexCoachU.com
Author, *The Art of Sex Coaching*

"It's Not About the Sex is a transformative guide for those in recovery from sexual compulsivity. Andrew's compassionate, forward-thinking book will help you begin and sustain meaningful connections. You will be deeply inspired by his uplifting insights as well as his own story."

Sandra Foster, PhD
Senior Faculty, College of Executive Coaching
Coauthor, *Positive Psychology in Coaching*

"Susskind does a superb job analyzing the emotional underpinnings of sexual addiction. I particularly enjoy his human, non-mechanistic approach."

Laurence Heller, PhD
Founder of the NeuroAffective Relational Model
Author, *Healing Developmental Trauma*

"This groundbreaking book fills a huge gap in helping sex addicts take the next steps toward sustainable, long-term recovery as they realize their fullest potential for intimacy."

Alexandra Katehakis, PhD
Author, *Sex Addiction as Affect Dysregulation*

"Focusing not only on behavior change, Susskind's inspiring approaches facilitate healing and recovery by addressing intimacy and development of deeper connection and meaning in relationships."

Larissa Mooney, MD
Assistant Clinical Professor, UCLA Department
of Psychiatry and Biobehavioral Sciences
Director, UCLA Addiction Medicine Clinic
Coeditor, *The Assessment and Treatment of Addiction*

"With sexual addiction, stopping compulsive behavior is only the first step in recovery. Sex addicts must also learn to live happier, healthier, more intimately connected lives. In *It's Not About the Sex*, Andrew Susskind provides a roadmap for living life to its fullest while healing from this debilitating addiction."

Robert Weiss, PhD, LCSW, CSAT-S
Author, *Sex Addiction 101, Out of the Doghouse,* and *Prodependence*

It's Not About the Sex

It's Not About the Sex

Moving from Isolation to Intimacy after Sexual Addiction

Andrew Susskind

CENTRAL RECOVERY PRESS

LAS VEGAS

Central Recovery Press (CRP) is committed to publishing exceptional materials addressing addiction treatment, recovery, and behavioral healthcare topics.

For more information, visit www.centralrecoverypress.com.

Publisher: Central Recovery Press
3321 N. Buffalo Drive
Las Vegas, NV 89129

24 23 22 21 20 19   1 2 3 4 5

Library of Congress Cataloging-in-Publication Data

Names: Susskind, Andrew (Social worker) author.
Title: It's not about the sex: moving from isolation to intimacy after
    sexual addiction / by Andrew Susskind, LCSW, SEP, CGP.
Other titles: It is not about the sex
Description: Las Vegas: Central Recovery Press, [2019]
Identifiers: LCCN 2018052579 (print) | LCCN 2019004243 (ebook) | ISBN
    9781949481075 (ebook) | ISBN 9781949481068 (pbk.: alk. paper)
Subjects: LCSH: Sex addiction. | Sexual desire disorders.
Classification: LCC RC560.S43 (ebook) | LCC RC560.S43 S87 2019 (print) | DDC
    616.85/833--dc23
LC record available at https://lccn.loc.gov/2018052579

Photo of Andrew Susskind by Starla Fortunato.

Cover design and interior by Deb Tremper of Six Penny Graphics.

To my grandmother, Rose Feingold, who traveled from Romania to Brooklyn to South Jersey. She believed in me when I needed it the most.

Table of Contents

The opposite of addiction is not sobriety.
The opposite of addiction is connection.
—Johann Hari

Introduction

Sexual addiction is commonplace in our culture. But so is the desire to heal. Twenty-five years ago, clients came to me with the sole purpose of stopping their self-destructive sexual behaviors. Today it's a different story: not only do they want to put an end to the cravings, they want to live better lives as well, with greater intimacy. The root cause of their suffering tends to be brokenheartedness. I have found that out-of-control sexual behavior is really about pain, and the remedy is reliable relationships.

It takes hitting bottom for many people to seek help, but even after therapy they're often vulnerable to relapse because they remain haunted by their past. On the outside, life looks stable. Yet on the inside there's a constant fear of backsliding. This is part of the sex addiction paradox: recovering addicts can appear high functioning while they deal with lingering pain, longing for meaningful connection.

While your compulsive sexual behavior likely began as a way to temporarily feel good, it eventually stopped working—and that's when you realized you had a serious problem. If you're sexually sober, but still feel stuck and dissatisfied, this book will help you establish sustainable ways to connect with others. It takes courage to ask for help, and perseverance to get unstuck, so I've provided steps in each chapter to guide you toward dependable relationships and emotional vitality.

There has never been a book fully devoted to life after sex addiction, and readers can find inspiration here in the stories of real people who've been in their shoes. These brave individuals fought through the compulsive urges, developing deeper relationships once the sexual acting out stopped. They've been in recovery for a long time, but the guidance they share goes well beyond their experiences at meetings or working the Twelve Steps. Now they live happy, imperfect lives, no longer defining themselves by past transgressions, instead pursuing meaningful contact with others.

As a psychotherapist, coach, and recovering sex addict who has been in twelve-step recovery for more than twenty-five years, I've witnessed hundreds of clients—and even some colleagues and friends—struggle with problematic sexual behavior and its consequences. They too have come to realize that sexual compulsivity is not about sex; it's about deep-rooted challenges with intimacy. I wrote this book for those moving beyond out-of-control sexual behavior and for the people helping them to heal from it.

Sex addiction thrives on isolation, shame, and secrecy. To diminish the stigma, this book contains the latest approaches the mental health field has to offer. It's been thirty-five years since Dr. Patrick Carnes released his groundbreaking book, *Out of the Shadows,* and this book builds upon that foundation. Drawing on Somatic Psychology, you'll gain perspective on what's going on in your nervous system and understand "somatic awareness," a method to calm your body and mind. Learning about Interpersonal Neurobiology, you'll see your tendencies toward fantasy and obsession through a new lens. With the help of Positive Psychology, you'll establish greater purpose in sobriety. All of which can lead to satisfying, intimate relationships.

Each chapter plants the seeds of purposeful connection. The goal is to move from intimacy avoidance to reliable relationships, from loss to gratitude, narcissism to generosity, shame to self-compassion, and codependency to clear boundaries. This book offers helpful step-by-step strategies to examine issues that hold readers back, such as unresolved grief, persistent perfectionism, and relentless fantasy, to name just a few.

Think of *It's Not About the Sex* as your gentle companion. It's meant to remind sex addicts that healing from the agonizing pain and isolation of compulsive sex requires daily practice and a new lifestyle. For sustainable recovery to take form, you'll need to say goodbye to your old ways and develop self-acceptance, empathy, and boundaries. It doesn't really matter if your pain is the cause or the effect of compulsive sex; it's time to move forward with purpose and direction. If you're up for this challenge, sexual compulsivity will finally be a part of your past.

In June 2018, the World Health Organization (WHO) announced the landmark decision to include "compulsive sexual behavior disorder" in the International Classification of Diseases (ICD-11). This is the first time in history sexual compulsivity has been recognized and validated as a mental health problem worthy of a diagnostic code. For decades there had been efforts to include "sexual addiction" as a diagnosis, to no avail.

Here's the dilemma. Does compulsive sexual behavior truly fit into the medical model of illnesses? Or is out-of-control sexual behavior an intimacy impediment caused by past trauma and brokenheartedness? I believe there can be a biological predisposition for compulsive behaviors, but trauma and childhood pain also play a significant role. In other words, whether it's nature or nurture we don't know for sure, but this recognition by the WHO will prompt more research and options for treatment, bringing hope to those still suffering.

Here's an illustration that opened my eyes to the distinctions between the terms sexual addiction and sexual compulsivity. My friend Tom, who is in his sixties, disclosed to me that after being molested as a teenager, he became sexually promiscuous in his twenties. He felt profoundly alone at the time, not knowing where to get help. In retrospect, Tom wouldn't have identified as a sex addict because it implies disease and illness, but he would've admitted to being sexually compulsive at the time. Ultimately, what counts is getting support. The twelve-step rooms work well for a lot of people. But there are those who never make it there.

Dr. Carnes, the original pioneer of this field, set the foundation for millions of people to get help for sexual addiction. Yet with as much as we've learned, I believe we still have a long way to go. In this book I chose to steer away from anything that pathologizes sexual behavior or describes it as a disease. The WHO classification is bittersweet because it finally legitimizes compulsive sexual behavior, yet identifying it as an illness ignores the roles childhood experience and trauma play. For the purposes of this book, I use several terms interchangeably: sex addiction, compulsive sex, out-of-control sexual behaviors, and self-destructive sexual behaviors. I welcome you to consider what fits you and what doesn't, based on your particular background or ongoing challenges.

Chapter One

Now What? Life after Sex Addiction

*I don't need anyone else to distract me from myself
anymore, like I always thought I would.*
—Charlotte Eriksson

If you are recovering from sexual addiction or sexual compulsion, you know how bad things got and how much better you feel now. But you hope this isn't as good as it gets. The decision to end this self-destructive behavior has opened the door to great possibilities, but it's not easy to achieve a balanced, connected, and meaningful life in recovery. The quest for sexual and emotional sobriety is an incredible growth opportunity. Yet how do you enter this new way of life? Initially, it took an internal shift—a conscious choice to move forward without self-sabotage—to decide once and for all that it was time to live your life more fully. This is similar to the first step of the twelve-step program: admitting compulsive sex is truly unmanageable. Finally, it was time to do something about your behavior.

Harm Reduction

Let's first acknowledge how sexual compulsion differs from substance abuse. I strongly believe that certain addictive, compulsive tendencies, such as sex, food, money, and work, require a harm-reduction approach. Wearing a condom instead of having unprotected sex is an example of harm reduction. Refraining from *all* sexual contact for an indefinite period of time is an example of the abstinence approach. Although both may be useful at times, rigid rules lead to dogmatic shaming and cause unnecessary pain, often resulting in relapse. Harm-reduction offers a variety of safer options rather than claiming there is only one way to get sexually sober.

The same principle applies to IV drug use. Needle-exchange programs are controversial yet effective examples of harm reduction. Providing clean syringes to drug abusers can save their lives, as the spread of disease is decreased. The drug user stays healthier longer, giving them more time to access the help they need. Similarly, the goal of sexual recovery is not to take a lifelong vow of celibacy. Most of you aren't monks—you're human beings who want real love and fulfilling sex.

As you heal from out-of-control sexual behaviors, over time you can introduce safer, healthier forms of sex and intimacy into your life. Temporary periods of abstinence from sexual contact may be necessary, but in the long run it's more realistic and productive to gradually integrate sex and love into your life. This book is meant to give you perspective on that hopeful journey, as well as practical strategies toward sustainable recovery.

Unfortunately, some of you are still silently suffering. In spite of your efforts, powerful emotions remain constricted while you long for a deeper connection with yourself and others. In recovery you hoped things would be different, but there's still an undercurrent of dissatisfaction. In this book, you'll hear from people in long-term recovery who've built bigger, better lives.

Let's look at what sexual sobriety means. Most twelve-step programs focusing on sex addiction suggest writing a recovery plan to clarify your sexual boundaries. A sponsor—someone who has worked the steps and has something that you admire and want for yourself—typically reviews the plan. This is how you set the parameters for your sexual sobriety.

A suggested sexual recovery plan might include three primary areas: bottom-line sexual behaviors or dangerous choices that you wish to abstain from completely; gray-area behaviors, which include risky actions that may lead to bottom-line behaviors but are not in themselves considered self-destructive; and top-line behaviors, which refer to life-affirming choices, such as quality time with loved ones and fun outdoor activities. Setting these boundaries is an example of harm reduction. These three categories are borrowed from the language of Sex and Love Addicts Anonymous (SLAA).

If you engage in bottom-line or gray-area behaviors, it's a sign that you're not entirely sexually or emotionally sober. For example, you may no longer contact escorts, but still obsessively spend time looking at call girl websites and masturbating to these images. This reduces harm, but is still compulsive sexual behavior. Yet the twelve-step program teaches you that it's about progress, not perfection. And because of the shame associated with sexual recovery, this philosophy holds even more weight.

Emotional Sobriety

So what exactly is emotional sobriety? At its core, it's the capacity to experience the fullness of life—a resilient, resourceful, and buoyant state of well-being when you feel most like yourself. Comfortable in your skin, you feel calm, relaxed, and at peace with who you are.

Speaking with people in recovery, you learn there are many different versions of emotional sobriety:

When do you feel most like yourself?

Susan: *When I'm creatively expressive. When I'm writing, when I'm singing, when I'm dancing, when I'm doing artwork, and when I'm public speaking.*

Robert: *While taking a long walk, being out in nature.*

Alex: *Running a few miles really makes me calmer. Meditation is also a reset button for me. A lot of times I get into a trance of suffering and then want to act out, but when I meditate, it's like I see it. I see what I'm doing and it's painfully obvious. It wakes me up.*

Colin: *When I'm consistently working my program, using the tools. When I'm not making somebody else or my job my Higher Power. When I'm with a friend who sees me and supports me and can be present and reflect with me— share their process and mine as well.*

Seth: *Before, I just couldn't realize it. I would just act out. A lot of times I didn't even know that I was feeling difficult feelings, and now I've learned that when I'm having difficult feelings they will pass over time. I'll go for a hike. I'll take my feelings to therapy. I may call a friend to talk it through.*

Part of my process is learning not to fight it and to just acknowledge it. Sometimes I literally say to myself, "The anxiety this morning just sucks." And it does. It feels crappy. But it passes.

When you were sexually compulsive, you often felt like you were crawling out of your skin—restless, desperate, and lonely. The good news is there's hope in becoming aware of your feelings. According to Dr. Tian Dayton, author of *Emotional Sobriety: From Relationship Trauma to Resilience and Balance,* these are the signs of emotional sobriety:

- Ability to regulate strong emotions
- Ability to regulate mood
- Ability to maintain a perspective on life circumstances
- Ability to regulate potentially harmful substances or behaviors
- Ability to live in the present
- Ability to regulate activity levels
- Ability to live with deep, intimate connection
- Resilience—the ability to roll with the punches

Before we take a closer look at the ingredients of emotional sobriety, let's define self-regulation. You may not be familiar with the term; it's a fairly new way to describe awareness of your internal state of being, based on your nervous system. The "self" refers to everything going on inside of you—emotions, moods, thoughts, and sensations. The "regulation" is how you achieve internal well-being to feel balanced, resilient, and most like yourself.

Dysregulation occurs when upsetting emotions are more powerful than your ability to calm yourself, such as when a partner breaks up with you. Of course this is upsetting, so how do you regulate more effectively? Strategies such as deep breathing, mindfulness, and asking for help will be explored throughout this book.

Ability to Regulate Strong Emotions

Self-regulation can be challenging in the best of times, especially if you're not sexually and emotionally sober. As you're working toward sexual sobriety, it's often difficult to identify what's going on inside you. As a result, self-regulation may not be possible yet. In this case, ask for support from others. Perhaps mutual regulation with a therapist can be a stepping-stone. When you *are* sober, your nervous system feels calmer and more grounded, and as a result you feel more like yourself. The good news about regulating your nervous system is that you'll begin to feel all of your feelings—the pleasant ones, the uncomfortable ones, and those in between.

Stressful or traumatic circumstances throw us all off. But ultimately, the dysregulation itself is not what matters so much as how you deal with it and find your way back to a regulated state. Learning to regulate your nervous system is a lifelong practice that can begin with somatic therapy.

When distressing events from your past were too traumatic to process at the time, the body stored these memories. The information comes out later in life in the way you fight, flee, or freeze during triggering events. Here is where "mind-body approaches" help you to regulate your nervous system and be aware of what's happening—what's known as "somatic awareness." Attending a mindfulness class, keeping a journal, and daily meditation will also help in the development of self-regulation skills.

Ability to Regulate Mood

Regulating your mood requires a tracking system. You wake up one morning and realize you don't want to get out of bed. This is the time for a self-assessment. Is it because you're still tired? Did you have a fight with your best friend last night? Are you trying to avoid some obligation? Is it difficult to pinpoint why you want to stay under the covers?

Identifying, tracking, and eventually regulating your mood is an ongoing practice of mindfulness and self-compassion that requires a healing team to be fully implemented; ideally, you'll have a therapist, sponsor, coach, friends, and family involved. You need people who are honest, direct, and offer unconditional love.

Because mood dysregulation may originate from your genetic predisposition or from past trauma, your first action step is to identify when it's happening and to ask for help from someone you can count on. The mere act of naming it and reaching out to others is healing in itself, because it takes you out of the isolation and shame often associated with moodiness.

Ability to Maintain a Perspective on Life Circumstances

In 1999, I was building my private practice and working part-time for a large managed healthcare company. It was too much for me, and I was on the verge of burnout. But I was fortunate enough to work with a coach who helped open up my outlook. Her optimistic, openhearted perspective was infectious, and over time I developed a new vision. This experience unlocked bigger, more creative possibilities and set the stage for my full-time private practice. As a result, I've carried more hope through the years, and I wouldn't have my fulfilling career if it wasn't for the seeds we planted together. This type of connection is not easy to find, but keep your eyes open for one loving person you can invite into your corner to bring a constructive perspective not possible on your own.

Building a brighter outlook is the cure for self-centered agonizing as well as a form of relapse prevention. As part of this process, you'll open up to the many possibilities in front of you, including asking for help and being of service to others.

Ability to Regulate Potentially Harmful Substances or Behaviors

Many of you reading this book likely choose to stay away from destructive behaviors. But emotional sobriety challenges you to take that a step further. In addition to staying away from dangerous activities, be vigilant about substances and actions that may be toxic for you. For instance, some may argue that in the grand scheme of things, sugar, flour, and caffeine aren't bad. The effects of these items are relatively benign in moderation. Yet these seemingly innocent substances impact your mood, energy, and even your sex drive.

Remain mindful of your exposure to anything that can throw off your emotional or physical sobriety, and start tracking these culprits. For instance, which of your relationships deplete you? How does money cause stress for you? What boundaries, or lack of boundaries, interfere with your recovery? What daily choices may become the slippery slope out of emotional sobriety?

Ability to Live in the Present

Age-old wisdom suggests that the here and now is the most fulfilling place to be. The past has passed and the future is unknown, so why not focus on the present, where you live 24/7? When my clients ask me what is significant about living in the present, I first share a warning: if you're used to spending a lot of time and energy focused on the past or future, it feels foreign to be fully yourself in the present. As a matter of fact, it's often uncomfortable at first, because it challenges you to truly live in the mind, body, and spirit of the moment. But the value of the present is that it's where you'll achieve a deeper connection with yourself and others. It's where love thrives. You're biologically wired for connection, so increasing your capacity for deeper contact and real love is a foundational step toward emotional sobriety and a fuller, more satisfying life.

The here and now may be unfamiliar territory for you. If so, meditation is a time-tested practice associated with being in the moment, and mindfulness strategies encourage you to observe the present from a nonjudgmental, curious lens. Keep in mind that anxiety pulls you toward the future and depression takes you into the past. Set the intention to practice here and now awareness and see what happens to your anxiety and depression. Of course, getting started is the hardest part. Consider trying a mindfulness meditation class or a meditation app to get the ball rolling.

Ability to Regulate Activity Levels

Family systems expert and best-selling author John Bradshaw uses the phrase "human beings versus human doings" to point out that well-being and balance require you to slow down. By creating a more thoughtful approach to how you invest your energy, you'll have a better chance at *being* rather than simply *doing*.

Being active can be life affirming, or yet another compulsion. Overscheduling activities might be a form of avoidance, or a way to connect and feel vital. Monitor these subtle differences to distinguish between life-depleting and life-enriching choices.

Our society values busyness. But leading a productive life is a trap if done in excess. Living a balanced life in recovery requires you to monitor your self-care habits, including sleep, nutrition, work, and sex. Keep a close eye on your use of time and energy, as well as how you prioritize or neglect your health. Self-neglect creates vulnerability to relapse, whereas self-care strengthens emotional sobriety.

Ability to Live with Deep, Intimate Connection

Intimacy and deeper connection are the primary focus of this book, but we'll explore this later on. Your challenge now is to cultivate openheartedness and emotional muscle building. Developing a greater capacity for love and intimacy is the ultimate goal of long-term sexual recovery, and improving your ability to give and receive love freely is a lifelong journey.

Resilience—Your Ability to Roll with the Punches

As mentioned before, you have the capacity to regulate yourself more efficiently, and there's a resilience zone that exists inside you where you feel most buoyant. We all have resources inside us; they may include a loving person, a favorite destination, or a warm, fuzzy memory. For example, my grandmother was the only loving and emotionally reliable person I could fully count on in my childhood. Even as I write this, I feel calmer. Although she died many years ago, my memory of her is a portable, tender resource that helps me feel regulated and resilient. These resources can be an inner touchstone to return to again and again in times of dis-ease.

Those of you who had problematic sexual behaviors in the past are not used to feeling resilient, so it takes practice to self-regulate. When resiliency grows, you'll experience a wider range of emotions, thoughts, and sensations. We'll explore resiliency and resourcing more fully later on. For now, simply pay attention to moments when you feel more like yourself and savor this state of well-being.

Ability to Regulate Behavior

This is the crème de la crème of emotional and sexual sobriety. No longer a victim of past compulsive behaviors, you stretch your muscles to explore a wider range of options.

So what's on your list of emotionally sober actions? What are your most nourishing relationships? How do you save money toward things that are personally enriching? What healthy foods do you like? What self-care choices can you prioritize? What sexual choices are fun and pleasurable for you? What improves you and what depletes you? Answering these questions will make you aware of the choices that either nurture or get in the way of your emotional sobriety. Every moment of every day you're making choices, and while this awareness may feel burdensome at first, eventually it leads to a resilient, regulated lifestyle.

But emotional sobriety requires sexual sobriety to succeed. When you're sexually sober, you'll automatically feel more resilient, yet when you're still sexually compulsive, you'll feel moody, disconnected, and dysregulated.

You used sexual compulsion as a survival strategy to cope with brokenheartedness. It served the purpose of distracting you from intense pain. Recovery, on the other hand, requires a belief that you will not only be okay, you'll find greater contentment than you would have if you did not let go of your former ways of coping.

Healing takes shape one moment at a time as you live in the here and now, in touch with your physical responses, thoughts, and feelings, and you begin to recognize the triggers from your past. By uncovering unconscious patterns and themes that date back to your childhood, you'll learn to make conscious choices in the present. And once you recognize your tendencies, you can never go back into denial about them. It's impossible for you to return to that old way of behaving when you move forward with clarity and vision.

Let's look at a real world example.

Case Study One: Jason's Emotional Sobriety

Jason is a thirty-two-year-old straight single male who is devoted to working his program on a daily basis. He's attended meetings for more than a year, and his life is much better for it. He's been able to hold a full-time job, he spends time with program friends, and he's sexually sober. But he doesn't feel *emotionally* sober.

"I work the steps, I have a sponsor, and I am a sponsor, and yet I still don't feel comfortable in my own skin," he admits. Despite the connections he's made at meetings, Jason remains isolated at times—socially awkward and anxious.

It's this state of dysregulation that calls for somatic awareness, self-regulation, and the tracking of what's causing his unease. Jason also needs to think carefully about his past. Where did his nervousness come from?

Growing up in a wealthy family and educated at a private school, Jason may appear at first glance to have had everything. His parents were both absent, though. Dad worked endless hours as a trial attorney, and Mom immersed herself in community organizations and social events. Most of Jason's time was spent with the nanny, leaving him starved for the love and attention of his parents. When he went away to boarding school, he learned that his father had engaged in multiple affairs, and soon thereafter his parents went through a contentious divorce.

Jason had all the material possessions he could want, but had felt utterly abandoned from a young age. He never experienced unconditional love or acceptance from his parents, the two people he most wanted to understand him. As a teen, he was moody and depressed. Feeling helpless, he didn't see how things could get any better. And that's when he discovered porn.

Through his first orgasm, Jason found a way to temporarily avoid the pain of isolation. Jason had no idea that pornography would be so intoxicating, and before he knew it, he was masturbating multiple times a day and expanding his consumption of porn in ways he would never have anticipated.

"I wanted to stop," he recalls. "I simply couldn't. Porn was my ally—my greatest distraction and escape. Instead of spending time with friends, I rushed home every day in search of new images that would give me a higher high."

It's been more than fifteen years since Jason became sexually compulsive. He's gone eighteen months now without porn, and because he's no longer using it to mute his feelings, his longing for a deep connection is more evident than ever. This terrifies Jason. But through the program and therapy, he's discovering the impact of his childhood pain and is ready to take a closer look at his enduring wounds.

Being emotionally abandoned at such a young age, in addition to the secrets and lies surrounding his father's infidelities, made trusting others a serious risk for Jason. But he realizes now that relying on dependable people is essential to living an emotionally sober life.

"My therapist and my sponsor are totally reliable," he says. "I've learned to ask for help, and they're always there for me. I feel like a work in progress and am more hopeful than before. Even my moods seem to be evening out, and sometimes I catch myself feeling gratitude and contentment."

Little by little, Jason is learning to identify and express his anger, fear, sadness, hurt, and joy honestly and directly. As a result, he's feeling more like himself more of the time.

"I know emotional sobriety requires daily attention and practice. It's a huge priority in my recovery, and in my life overall."

Although Jason has barely left the starting gate, he envisions a future in which he feels calmer, more peaceful, and more grounded—an internal experience he's never known before.

When you're sexually and emotionally sober, time and resources become liberated. No longer wasting precious energy on destructive sexual behavior, you reawaken neglected passions, which provides you with a meaningful life. During the seven years Alex has been in recovery, his awareness has expanded exponentially. Now he sees himself more clearly—with choice rather than limitations. He makes thoughtful decisions about sex and relationships, as well as bold career moves. Thanks to his quest for growth, he moved from feeling stuck to feeling expansive:

> *I didn't really know myself before. One of the hallmarks of the twelve-step program is to develop a meaningful relationship with yourself. It became apparent that it's not just about the sex. Certain things started to open up. I changed careers because I was living a very self-absorbed life. That would not have happened if it wasn't for therapy and twelve-step work.*

Colin shared a similar trajectory:

> *Since getting sober, I've gotten into grad school, started a career that I enjoy, achieved a deeper connection with friends, deeper relationships with my family, and have seen clinical depression lift after twenty plus years. Every aspect of my life has been transformed.*

Alex and Colin demonstrate the growth available in long-term recovery. You'll hear more from them as we continue to explore healing opportunities that present themselves.

In psychoanalysis, it's believed that people defend against their greatest needs, which is a universal intimacy dilemma. It's human nature to long for love and a deeper connection, yet to avoid it at the same time for fear of rejection. A tension exists between these opposing forces, but there's also aliveness in this conflict—an awareness of your longings and your fears.

The universal desire for connection is a biological drive that likely dates back to our species' early days surviving in cooperative tribes. Humans are social creatures, but that evolutionary instinct is stymied by addictive, compulsive behaviors. Sexual compulsion is a misguided attempt to get what you really want—a secure attachment with someone you can count on. The internal wrestling match applies to everyone—all of us are biologically wired for connection. Yet compulsive sex creates distance from your emotional longings and turns into intimacy avoidance.

Revealing Blind Spots

Sex addicts compartmentalize sex and intimacy as separate experiences, so the quest to integrate them may seem like a long haul. Similar to how a drug addict chooses to abstain from their substance of choice, you've chosen to give up the adrenaline rush and immediate gratification that accompanied risky behaviors like anonymous sex or visits to "happy ending" massage parlors. If you can maintain sexual sobriety, an open heart, and some perseverance, all the rewards of emotional sobriety may come your way too.

Which is not to say the process is easy. Compulsive sex was likely a secretive part of you. To share it with others is scary, yet also a powerful way to be more transparent and courageous. One of the challenges over time is to integrate both the shadow and the light within you. It felt shameful and deceptive to engage in socially unacceptable behavior. On the other hand, at times it was playful and exciting. Bringing these sides of you together and into the light, slowly and respectfully—accepting and understanding all parts of yourself—is an essential part of long-term healing. This usually happens with a therapist or a sponsor, and ultimately results in you feeling fully seen and heard, without compartmentalizing.

The sexual risks and secrecy of your past can be replaced with emotional risks and vulnerability from now on. All it takes is the daily intention of willingness, transparency, and courage. Love and intimacy is not just a concept—it's a practice. You may still want to regulate the emotional distance between yourself and others, but you'll always be wired for connection as well, and therein lies the dilemma.

Once you begin to face your avoidant style, you'll feel awkward and discouraged at first, but over time you'll get to experience the dividends of deeper connection. Aware of the contributors to your pain—grief, shame, self-centeredness, and a lack of boundaries—you'll finally see these tendencies for what they are—ways of shielding yourself that have outlasted their purpose. Alex illustrates this internal shift as follows:

> *In recovery I got to see things about myself that I'd never seen, like when I want to act out, when I don't, how much I push people away, and how I cling to people. I was so self-absorbed... I decided to change careers to be of service to others.*

One of the most gratifying parts of my practice is witnessing clients go from being unconscious to conscious. When we first meet, they know they are in pain but aren't sure why. As we work together to shine a light on past patterns, they come to understand themselves, and feel freedom and relief as a result. When past triggers become less powerful, the here and now becomes a more tolerable and even pleasant place to be. At last, you feel more comfortable in your skin.

Entering the Here and Now

Sometimes you'll hear an old-timer at a twelve-step meeting tell a newcomer, "Do what's in front of you and let go of the results." This age-old advice is about taking things one moment at a time when life feels overwhelming. It removes future expectations, to focus on the here and now.

What's so great about living in the present? It's where your life force is most accessible—an oasis of emotional sobriety is available there. In fact, resiliency and buoyancy only exist in the here and now. But it takes mental muscle for you to breathe into each moment, and until now that muscle has been only infrequently used. Later on, we'll take a deeper look at ways you can stretch this mindfulness muscle to achieve less self-judgment and more self-acceptance.

In twelve-step rooms you also hear a lot about faith and hope. This may feel foreign to you, but without optimism, recovery is a constant struggle. Developing a working relationship with hope requires patience. The good news is that faith will reveal itself over time if you're patient.

You'll need to strengthen your capacity to trust and rely on other people too. Before recovery, it was scary to depend on others because of the hurt and disappointment that likely occurred in your past. It takes practice to ask for help from people, but eventually it becomes a habit that results in less anxiety and loneliness. By learning to take risks and rely on a sponsor, coach, or therapist, for example, you carve out new neural pathways in your brain that let you know trust and intimacy is not only possible, but preferable to acting out. Hope, faith, and trust are vital elements for you to experience more meaningful connection.

The term "sex addiction" entered the clinical community less than four decades ago, and we're still learning how it works and how to heal from it. Yes, we've come a long way, but I believe that for as much as we do know, a lot remains unclear. One of my primary motivations for writing this book was to share an unexplored perspective with you: mainly, that the challenges of long-term sex addiction recovery offer great opportunities to learn about yourself through the integration of sex, love, and intimacy.

Action Steps:

1. Hope requires practice. Write a list of memories and experiences during which you felt hopeful. Now take stock and write down anything in your life that gives you hope.

2. Developing deeper connections to those you trust is a requirement of recovery. Emotionally reliable relationships are essential, as they move you away from isolation and your former way of life. Name the dependable people that existed in your past. Now, name reliable people in your life today. If you have difficulty identifying any, name the people who you would like to count on more.

3. Emotional sobriety requires you to live in the here and now, which brings freedom from worry for the future and anxiety about the past. Answer the question in the Emotional Sobriety section of

this chapter and list a few realistic action steps to support your emotional sobriety.

4. Eliminating self-protective, medicating behaviors won't kill you. And embracing vulnerability may be hard at first, but you'll learn ways to connect more deeply with others. What tools do you have in your intimacy toolbox right now? What tools would you like to add?

5. It's not the dysregulation that matters—it's how you choose to manage it. In recovery you're an imperfect, lovable human being. Track your dysregulated states against your more regulated states of resiliency and well-being. Keep in mind that you're teaching your nervous system new ways to react to unpleasant, disturbing situations.

6. Change takes muscle and perseverance, and self-awareness and self-understanding create the possibility for external change. If you're navigating a ship on the high seas and you turn the wheel slightly, you'll end up at a completely different destination from where you planned. What is a small change you can make today that will make a big difference?

Chapter Two

The Gratitude of Loss

*Life seems sometimes like nothing more than
a series of losses, from beginning to end.
That's the given. How you respond to those
losses, what you make of what's left,
that's the part you have to make up as you go.*
—Katharine Weber

Grief is a good thing. Don't get me wrong. Grieving is really hard work, but ultimately it's a path to better understand buried parts of yourself.

In American culture, it's taboo to spend too much time and energy dwelling on loss. Instead, you're encouraged to get over it and move on with your life. During the course of your recovery, you'll face a series of losses, and each of them is a growth opportunity within itself. In spite of the heavy emotional work required, I invite you to explore and process your grief, because it's a prime opportunity to learn about a valuable part of yourself.

Doors Opening, Doors Closing

A lot of celebration takes place around new beginnings such as weddings and births, but the dying process and the grief that follows typically get overshadowed. This version of denial can get in the way of recognizing the countless losses that go along with your history of out-of-control sexual activities.

In the early 1990s, I worked as a hospice social worker visiting terminally ill patients and their families. It was a privilege to be invited into someone's home during these sacred moments. As a part of that openhearted, loving hospice team, I absorbed valuable life lessons that have stayed with me ever since:

- Death, dying, and loss are sacred experiences
- The dying process is unpredictable, uncertain, and often hidden from view
- Individuals facing their final days, weeks, or months often bring great wisdom and perspective to the living

What does any of this have to do with sex addiction? Facing the end of your relationship with compulsive sex is a similarly sacred experience if you remain open to its lessons. For those interviewed in this book, spiritual exploration helped provide meaning as sexual compulsion faded. The losses opened their hearts to new purpose—a vital element to sustainable recovery. Spirituality can be defined as "whatever gives your life meaning." You get to define it for yourself, and whatever your belief system, that blank canvas reveals itself during moments of grief. Stay open to this possibility and you'll discover a spiritual connection inside you.

Saying goodbye to an addiction is a unique loss, and there's a lot of uncertainty and unpredictability that go along with sobriety. Addictive, compulsive behaviors are attempts to feel better, so it's scary to give them up. It makes you vulnerable. Addictions are also used to regulate your nervous system, so it's crucial to build and strengthen new, effective ways to cope as you give up destructive behaviors.

Fortunately, your compulsions only worked for so long. Then came the courage to let them go in hopes that something better would replace these habits. If you learn to live with the uncertainty of the future and the feelings that go along with the unknown, you're on your way toward long-lasting recovery.

Grief has been one of my greatest teachers, and I believe it can be yours as well. When three of my family members died in three consecutive years, I reached out for the love around me and realized I was not alone. I experienced resiliency and intimacy in a way I'd never imagined. As a wise chaplain once told me, it's not what you do or say at the end of someone's life, it's about your "ministry of presence." When I witnessed loss, I offered my clients a healing space for grief to be experienced and expressed. Saying goodbye to sex addiction also requires attention to the losses, and there are many. Like all other emotional experiences, loss is a parade; sometimes it stalls, at other times it moves slowly, but it always passes.

Saying goodbye to someone you love is particularly complicated. While my mom was fighting end-stage lung cancer, we had seven months to make up for lost time. Although it was never spoken, we knew our time together was ending. This was a rare opportunity to connect more deeply before she died. She lived more than a hundred miles away, yet I did my best to show up consistently and openheartedly, often with my faithful cocker spaniel Cooper in tow. I knew my mother loved me, but she didn't know how to love me the way I wanted. As a child, I tried desperately to get her attention and please her. No matter how hard I tried, I always fell short. As a young adult, my search for sex and love became out of control as I looked for validation wherever I could find it.

In spite of our complicated history, I did my best to show up for her in her final months without expectations. Instead of the usual tension, we shared moments of humor, ease, and tenderness that were never possible in our relationship before this pending loss. Letting go of the fantasy mother I wanted brought us closer.

Breaking up with Your Addiction

Just as there is labor with birth, there is labor with death. When you make an active choice to say goodbye to sexual compulsion, the process of letting go is not a single event. It begins when your pain has become intolerable, often referred to as *hitting bottom*. First you stop the obvious high-risk behaviors, but later on in recovery you might also halt the more subtle behaviors, like keeping secrets from your partner or seeking sexual validation from others. Grieve these compulsive tendencies as you let go of them to make room for deeper connection and contentment.

That's right: *hitting bottom* is a type of death. The death of a coping style. The death of a survival strategy. The death of a double life. Afterward comes grief, which opens up emotional space to build a multidimensional recovery. So how do you consciously grieve this loss?

You've all heard unhelpful platitudes, like "you'll get over it," and "time heals all wounds." The loss of your compulsion is not something to "get over," but rather something to learn to live with and understand. In examining the underlying layers of loss that predate your out-of-control sexual behaviors, you may discover what contributes to your compulsivity. Be patient with yourself as you unearth these past experiences. Trying to get over your losses too quickly can lead to relapse, but exploring the losses safely and productively allows you to integrate rather than hide from them. Accept yourself fully for exactly who you are, and similarly, grieve losses of the past for exactly what they are—pain that accumulated over many years. Let's look at the example of a man named Kevin.

Case Study Two: Kevin's Grief

When Kevin turned fifty, he finally recognized life was passing him by. He owned a local gym and felt proud of this accomplishment, but as he aged, he grew progressively lonelier and emptier. Married and divorced three times, Kevin now attributes his failed marriages to his inability to remain faithful. He had one affair after another, countless illicit massage parlor trips, and too many prostitutes to remember.

"I don't want to spend the second half of my life the way I did the first," Kevin told me. "I have to stop chasing and find a way to be happy." His parents were highly successful professionals—his father an orthopedic surgeon and his mother a high school principal. There was love in the home, but his parents struggled to express it. Most of the time, he felt criticized and judged, leaving him feeling inferior and stupid. From a very young age, Kevin was pressured to excel in school, but he was not a good student. In high school he was diagnosed with Attention Deficit Disorder and learning disabilities. He felt like a total disappointment to his parents, especially in contrast to his overachieving sister. But in the local gym he found a refuge and worked hard to build his body.

When Kevin didn't reach his physical goals, he started taking steroids and abusing Adderall. He participated in bodybuilding competitions and received a lot of compliments on his physique. Though it was not his parents' idea of success, Kevin enjoyed feeling seen and validated.

Fast-forward a few decades and Kevin is now receiving a wake-up call. He not only lost a marriage to divorce, but also lost custody of his baby girl, who was recently diagnosed with leukemia. His daughter's health crisis led Kevin to find sexual and emotional sobriety. "I don't know how I'm going to live without the shenanigans," he admits, "but I do know I can't live this way anymore."

It's always impossible to predict the moment someone like Kevin will finally choose to give up his sexual exploits. In this case, he was brokenhearted to have such limited time with his two-year-old daughter. He didn't want to abandon her emotionally the same way he had felt abandoned by his parents. Kevin wants to break the family legacy.

On the one hand, his sexual transgressions have been a survival strategy. He felt strong and successful as a bodybuilder who could get women's attention on a daily basis, and even built a career around this deep longing for admiration. Beneath these efforts, though, was a lonely boy wishing to be cherished and loved, and he realizes now that he has to change. If he wants to be there for his little girl, he needs to say goodbye to the compulsive sexual behavior once and for all.

"It's taken me much longer than I would have wished, but I want to live a life of integrity and be a dependable father," he says. "I know it's too late to fix my marriages, but my kid deserves more, and I want to do whatever it takes to finally say goodbye to the secrets and lies."

Processing grief can be lonely and emotionally raw. What you need to do in a situation like Kevin's is lean on dependable people who understand you. It's vital that you break out of the habit of isolation.

Who can you count on in your life? Who can you rely on emotionally at a time of loss? You don't need a lot of people. As a matter of fact, you can start with one person, but identifying a handful of people over time is a key to grief work, shame reduction, and ultimately sustainable recovery.

Grief comes in waves large and small, and riding these waves builds a capacity to process grief effectively. In her pioneering work studying death, psychiatrist Elisabeth Kübler-Ross identified the five stages of loss as denial, anger, bargaining, depression, and acceptance. But regarding the duration, form, and intensity of these stages, grief is unpredictable, with lots of ups and downs along the way. This applies to the grieving of sexually compulsive behaviors as well. Don't go through this affliction alone.

What made it possible for you to say goodbye to your addiction?

Colin: *Using the tools of twelve-step recovery, which meant getting a sponsor, working the steps, making outreach calls, and going to regular meetings. I could not kick the addiction on my own no matter how hard I tried.*

Alex: *I was just really tired of it… like the STDs and the shame. I got really sick of myself—the behaviors and the feelings were unbearable.*

Susan: *I needed twelve-step recovery. I needed one-on-one talk therapy. I also went to a trauma group. I lived in a rehab center for fifteen months, and that was the biggest boost out of prostitution for me.*

Stages of Grief
Denial

Looking more closely at the five stages of grief, we begin with denial, a universal coping strategy. When something is too overwhelming to comprehend in the moment, denial is where we hang out until we're ready to move forward. It protects you so you don't have too much to process at once. As a result, loss gets buried inside until you're ready to address it.

Leaving behind all compulsive behaviors is hard to do all of a sudden. Because these adrenaline-filled experiences were a reliable way to cope for many years, your destructive strategies may need to fade gradually. Remember, saying goodbye to your acting-out behaviors means letting go of a long-term relationship—possibly one of the longest you've ever known. Breaking through denial is a delicate process, so prepare to recognize stubborn parts of your compulsive mind that require extra time to let go.

Anger

Anger is often misunderstood as a negative emotion, when in fact it serves a powerful purpose in your emotional sobriety. Anger is a force to protect yourself as you decide what is unacceptable. By saying "no" or "stop," you'll establish clear boundaries and know where you end and the other person begins. In the future, anger will help you make room for a big "yes" for the things you choose to do. When you express anger safely and productively, it creates direct, honest contact and brings you closer to others.

Anger is inevitable in life and recovery. You'll likely direct it toward yourself, toward others, toward a sponsor, even toward God. Let the anger breathe, and process it safely through step work, therapy, or workshops that teach you how anger can be safe and productive. Keep in mind that anger turned inward fuels depression, so expressing anger can actually be your anti-depressant.

Bargaining

I've always loved bargaining. As a kid, I would go to garage sales with my mom, an antique dealer, and she'd show me the art of negotiation. She taught me to never accept the sticker price. If an item cost three dollars, I would offer them two. When it comes to loss, bargaining may be an internal deliberation, or bartering with a Universal Power, as in, "Why do I have to quit again? But why now? Can I just do it once more?"

These questions may have been indulged in the past, when you first considered giving up your acting-out behaviors. They also bring forth spiritual questions, such as "Who am I now that I'm sober?" Choosing a life in sobriety is a tremendous identity shift, so try to stay humble during the transition and keep in mind that for as much as you now know, there's just as much that you don't know.

Depression

Sadness, a natural response to loss, is often confused with clinical depression. Feeling melancholy is understandable, and by experiencing the full range of grief, you'll process your losses more thoroughly. There's no right or wrong way to express grief—you might choose to hibernate at times, or rather prefer to be around others. During the transition from sexual compulsion to sobriety, it's essential to give yourself time and space to experience withdrawal. But safety comes first. If depression progresses to helplessness, hopelessness, or suicidal thoughts, seek immediate professional attention.

Acceptance

The practice of acceptance is suggested in the Big Book of Alcoholics Anonymous, as well as in Buddhism and other wise ancient traditions. Accepting yourself for who you are at any given time is a lifelong practice. Accepting others for who they are is also a daily effort. The more you're able to accept life in the present—not dwell on the past or future—the more emotionally sober you'll feel. Living fully in the here and now may not be possible right away, but it's a realistic long-term goal if you're up for the challenge.

In recovery from sexual compulsion, fondly recalling memories of acting out, while forgetting or overlooking the negative consequences, is known as *euphoric recall*. Learning to say goodbye to the high associated with euphoric recall is key to building sustainable recovery. This is an inevitable part of sobriety, as past images linger in the pathways of your brain. Over time these memories will become mere echoes of your past, rather than unwelcome invaders. When euphoric recall is awakened, consider it your recovery alarm clock ringing. Establish a different relationship with the slideshows of your past behavior as you develop new neural pathways of connection and love.

If sexual compulsion has left you with a frozen heart, early recovery is like a thawing process. The melting happens gradually; it can't be rushed with the aid of a blowtorch. Set up a few solid pillars of support—emotionally dependable people you can contact when feeling raw and vulnerable in your grief.

In his workbook *Facing the Shadow*, Dr. Patrick Carnes suggests you put together a list of realistic, contrary actions available for when you have the urge to act out. The compulsive part of you is used to solitude and secrecy, so a plan to combat temptation during moments of isolation is wise. This will also get you thinking about how to create connections. It can't be stressed enough how important it is that you move toward dependable people and exit your emotional quarantine as you grieve. Being alone in your pain is familiar territory. But let the wisdom of others lead you toward more profound self-acceptance and self-understanding.

What do you identify as your greatest loss due to sexual compulsion?

Seth: *The loss of time with my family, especially while my children were growing up.*

Colin: *Wasted time. A good decade of my life could have been more productive.*

Mario: *Time. The regret is that I could have accomplished more if I used that time for something else.*

Alex: *A sense of personal connection with somebody else. I'm not good at emotionally connecting with others, but I'm really good at sexually connecting.*

Susan: *I had two abortions—both when I was much younger—and now that I'm forty-eight I can't have children. That's the biggest loss for me.*

Losing time, losing connection, losing the chance to have children—these are poignant reminders of the stakes of sexual compulsion. By listing your specific losses and missed opportunities, you'll create a heightened awareness of your grief, and in turn begin the process of self-compassion and self-forgiveness. Therapists, sponsors, and trusted confidants are typically the best partners for respectfully grieving these losses with you.

Grieving the Loss of the Fantasy

In my psychotherapy practice, a universal theme is *grieving the loss of the fantasy*—saying goodbye to the wish for a storybook childhood once and for all. This longing for an ideal environment often takes place as soon as we exit our mother's womb. Maybe you didn't want to leave its perfect warmth and nutrients, but having outgrown it, you fought your way through the birth canal and entered the world, a place that has proved less than ideal.

Now, you don't literally want to go back in the womb, but you do wish to be seen and understood in the right way, at the right time, with ideal warmth. As children, some of you received generous *attunement*. That is to say, the attention you received included listening, understanding, and empathy—"tuning in" in a sincere way. Others of you were neglected. But in any case, there's always a gap between what you wished was available and what actually occurred. This dilemma existed as soon as you entered the world. *Grieving the loss of the fantasy* is the process of accepting your past and stepping into the reality of your life and recovery today.

Typically, recovery from sexual compulsion means grieving three distinct losses:

1. Letting go of the high of acting out compulsive behaviors.
2. Letting go of the fantasy of an ideal childhood
3. Letting go of the love addict's vision of how a relationship should be (as portrayed in films like *Sleepless in Seattle* or *Beauty and the Beast*)

Pia Mellody, a codependency and love addiction expert, describes love addiction as a "relational pattern that's rooted in obsession with fantasy or the desire to be rescued." Many of you need to acknowledge that love addiction is a problem and grieve its loss. This is one of the greatest hurdles for sex addicts, love addicts, and love avoidants, yet it's necessary in order to heal from the deeper suffering.

As I reflect on my own attachment patterns, I recognize a tendency toward love avoidance and distancing, but it hasn't been a life sentence. I may always have lingering challenges fully leaning into genuine love and intimacy, but fortunately, as recovery deepens, this pattern becomes less intrusive and more an echo of my past.

Recovery is about healing past wounds as much as it is about addiction. What have you done to grieve your childhood losses?

Alex: *You think you get a layer down, then another one comes up. For me, it's required a lot of therapy. There are many unprocessed emotions that surface. Feeling like a child again, going through extreme anger—for me, the challenge is to stay in those moments and not suppress them or act them out sexually.*

Mario: *More therapy to learn how to honor my imperfections.*

Colin: *Going through the steps. I've also gone through periods of crying and grieving and prayer for healing along the way.*

Seth: *I've been in therapy for years and have done deep work around my losses. Some early trauma fueled my addiction, which I didn't understand then. There were feelings I had numbed out or didn't appreciate. Grieving comes out through my step work, journaling, and workshop retreats.*

Susan: *I've written about it, written about it, and written about it some more, and I talked about it aloud to my sponsor, so I've had it witnessed by another human being and shared it with God.*

Susan emphasizes the remarkable healing power of words, specifically the reparative quality of sharing your writing with a trusted confidant.

Journaling is a productive tool for processing thoughts, feelings, and traumatic experiences. Considering the magnitude of grief work, the more outlets you have for self-expression, the better.

Letter to Your Sex Addiction

In my workbook *From Now On: Seven Keys to Purposeful Recovery*, I suggest a writing exercise called "Letter to Your Addiction." For some people, putting highly private and deeply shameful memories down on paper is the safest way to access them. Writing offers absolute freedom to express yourself without censorship. This exercise suggests that you divide the letter into two parts. The first part focuses on gratitude for your addiction; the second part is to say goodbye to it. Your out-of-control sexual behavior served a purpose once, and it's okay to acknowledge your gratitude for it. Meanwhile, putting your goodbye to sexual compulsion into words gives you the opportunity to say whatever you want to say to it. The letter can be postcard sized or several single-spaced pages. I suggest you find an inspirational space where you feel creative. When I do therapeutic writing, I generally go to a hiking trail or favorite beach where I can slow down and make room for whatever comes up. The idea is to let the words flow without editing.

But how can gratitude and grief coexist? Because grief is an inevitable part of life and recovery, I strongly advise that you embrace it as a healing experience rather than another layer of shame. You can see loss as an adversary or make it your ally in recovery. Practicing gratitude—and please take note of the word *practicing*—is a counterbalance to the emotional work associated with grief and loss. Eventually, when you become grateful for your losses, you know you're on a track toward deeper healing.

For six years in the 1990s, I facilitated a weekly bereavement group at a hospital in Los Angeles. Most of the members were widows and widowers, but there were also siblings, adult children, and other loved ones. All of them showed up at a time of deep sorrow and existential crises. They attended because they wanted to feel less alone, more hopeful, and eventually be of service to others going through what they'd experienced. Week in and week out, they embodied resiliency and buoyancy. Their specific losses became a part of them rather than defining them. By showing up consistently, developing camaraderie, and drawing on faith that revealed itself in unexpected ways, their losses shifted in the direction of freedom, hope, and compassion. The same goes for recovery from sexual compulsion.

At the end of every group, I would ask someone to read the following affirmation which applies to all losses—both a loved one's death and saying goodbye to an addiction:

An Affirmation for Those Who Have Lost
by James E. Miller

I believe there is no denying it: it hurts to lose.
It hurts to lose a cherished relationship with another,
Or a significant part of one's own self.
It can hurt to lose that which has united one with the past
Or that which has beckoned one into the future.
It is painful to feel diminished or abandoned,
To be left behind or left alone.
Yet I believe there is more to losing than just the hurt and the pain.
For there are other experiences that loss can call forth.
I believe that courage often appears,
However quietly it is expressed,
However easily it goes unnoticed by others.
The courage to be strong enough to surrender,
The fortitude to be firm enough to be flexible.
I believe a time of loss can be a time of learning unlike any other,
And that it can teach some of life's most valuable lessons.

In the act of losing there is something to be found.
In the act of letting go, there is something to be grasped.
In the act of saying "goodbye" there is a "hello" to be heard.
For I believe living with loss is about beginnings as well as endings.

And grieving is a matter of life more than death.
And growing is a matter of mind and heart and soul more
        than of body.
And loving is a matter of eternity more than of time.
Finally, I believe in the promising paradoxes of loss.

In the midst of darkness, there can come great Light.
At the bottom of despair, there can appear a great Hope.
And deep within loneliness, there can dwell a great Love.
I believe these things because others have shown the way
Others who have lost and have then grown through their losing,
Others who have suffered and then found new meaning.
So I know I am not alone; I am accompanied, day after night, night
        after day.

This poem always touches me for the way it acknowledges hopelessness and hope, darkness and light. It speaks to the human spirit moving forward to rediscover purpose and direction. Every week, the bereavement group inspired me with its members' deep connection to loved ones lost, and the determination and resiliency each person demonstrated. In the same way, sexual recovery reveals the resourcefulness of the human spirit. You get to integrate the past while rebuilding your life inside and out.

Recovery opens up more time in your life since you're not acting out. What do you do with the time you now have?

Robert: *I'm more present in the things I do. It's opened horizons to pursue things I truly enjoy, such as being out in nature, hiking, skiing, cycling, and yoga—things that have to do with body, mind, and spirit.*

Mario: *I'm enjoying singing in a chorus now.*

Colin: *My life is so rich and full. I've been able to attend grad school and be more productive at work. The number of friends in my life has greatly expanded. I'm able to go out and have fun.*

Seth: *I went back to school. I put a lot more time into my relationship, and we do a lot of things together as a result of that. I play guitar. I read more. I go dancing. I do some writing. I spend time with my kids and friends.*

Susan: *I have a life now. I go do yoga. I attend lots of parties. I do karaoke. I get to have fun! It's such a joy. Dancing, cooking. I think the biggest thing is showing up for people at their events and having events of my own. It's so great.*

Remember grief isn't something to get over. You learn to live with it—to integrate rather than compartmentalize. Long-term recovery from sexual compulsion challenges you to combine sex with intimacy, to move from secrecy and shame to transparency and self-compassion, and all of these adaptations require a conscious internal shift.

New beginnings are intimidating, but they can also be the most fulfilling times of your life if you're willing to build a solid infrastructure for recovery. I recently talked to a client who had been engaging in anonymous sex for more than thirty years and now acknowledges that he is sick and tired of this lifestyle. I told him this was a prime opportunity to grieve. Though he looked cynical at first, he realized he wasn't alone. I was going to be with him as he said farewell to his double life. He has no idea what lies ahead, but knows it's time to lay the past to rest and grieve his losses.

Action Steps:

1. Grief is a challenge unlike any other, and saying goodbye to the sexual compulsion requires great faith. On a scale of one to ten, ask yourself how willing you are to grieve the loss of your sex addiction.
2. Bottoming out feels like a death, but it can also be a portal to getting to know parts of yourself you didn't know existed. Write about your experience of hitting bottom and its significance to your recovery today.
3. Grief comes in waves big and small. Learn to ride the waves to make it back to shore safely. Write about a recent loss and how you

navigated it. Who was there for you? How did you feel after the waves subsided?

4. Kübler-Ross's stages of grief include denial, anger, bargaining, depression, and acceptance. Identify a sex-addiction-related loss and the stages of grief you experienced with it.

5. Regret is part of recovery. Coming to terms with it unburdens you from the past and creates more freedom. List your biggest regrets and assign an action step you can take to grieve each of them.

Chapter Three

Turning down the Volume on Shame

If we can share our story with someone who responds with empathy and understanding, shame can't survive.
—Brené Brown

Shame gets in your way if not processed fully. It registers as something wrong with you, rather than an action that was wrongful. Beginning as a painful event, it is stored as a character defect. So although shame can be experienced as an emotion or thought, it leaves its imprint in your body, as trauma specialist Babette Rothschild noted in her influential book, *The Body Remembers.* Feelings of shame are stored physically through your brain-body connection, and can result in panic attacks, migraines, irritable bowel syndrome, and other symptoms.

Because the shame associated with problematic sexual behavior is often buried, it is yet another form of the secrets and lies that accompany sex addiction. For example, a client used to hire prostitutes, but was a deacon in his church. His profound shame resulted in him keeping this secret for years. Although he was a leader in his religious community, he lived a double life and felt completely disconnected from his wife and loved ones. By identifying and talking about shame, you can minimize this isolation, secrecy, and other harmful side effects.

You may use the terms *shame* and *guilt* interchangeably, but there's an important distinction between the two. You feel guilt for what you *do*; you feel shame for who you *are*. The internal experience of shame is more profound than guilt: It goes to the heart of your identity. You become disillusioned with yourself, because sex addiction is incongruent with your personal values.

Illuminating Shame

In 1988, John Bradshaw introduced the concept of developmental shame and the inner child to the mainstream public through his groundbreaking book *Healing the Shame that Binds You*. Bradshaw reminded us that we enter the world with a precious innocence, but then toxic shame seeps in. He was among the first clinicians to introduce *inner child work*, an exploration of your childhood innocence, as an opportunity for shame reduction. Children are inherently playful, loving, and spontaneous, and Bradshaw encourages you to find a way back to those qualities to reclaim your vitality. Your inner critic and self-loathing parts of you diminish as you heal from shame wounds—an essential component of sustainable long-term recovery.

When Bradshaw popularized the term *inner child*, he changed the conversation about addiction forever. Building more compassion for the quiet, suffering kid inside you decreases your vulnerability to relapse. As you identify and explore the themes and patterns of your turbulent childhood, you'll build awareness and empathy for the suffering you've endured.

All of us want to be seen, heard, understood, respected, and valued. In the past you sexualized these unmet needs instead of processing them, and acting out these longings in turn produced shame. When a person's childhood isn't safe and unconditionally loving, they often play emotional catch-up, attempting to reclaim what wasn't available then.

Healthier Shame vs. Toxic Shame

Healthier shame is like an internal alarm bell that lets you know when you've crossed a boundary or are too walled off. Ideally, it's part of your broader conscience that keeps you out of trouble. Unfortunately, a hallmark of sexual compulsion is the inability to know your limits, or a tendency to reject them. When you started to realize your sexual behaviors were unmanageable, you likely wanted to stop them but couldn't. Crossing boundaries, intruding on others' personal space, and not knowing how to cease high-risk behaviors are signs of rampant sex addiction. Establishing clear standards of behavior is the key to healing your healthy shame detection system. Clear boundaries are also crucial to establishing respect, trust, and intimacy with other people.

In recent years, renowned author and social scientist Dr. Brené Brown has done groundbreaking research into shame. Her 2010 TEDx talk, "The Power of Vulnerability," presented shame as the fear of disconnection. In general, sex addicts are terrified of authentic connection, vulnerability, and emotional risk-taking. Sustainable recovery takes shape when you step outside of fear and courageously move toward real intimacy.

How exactly does this relate to out-of-control sexual behavior? Toxic shame is often the cause as well as the effect of the problem. Your inner child carries shame, which sets you up to withdraw and act out as an adult. Sexual acting out is socially taboo, so you blend in secrets and lies, leading to a double life—one you show others, and one that becomes your "shadow," or addict self. On the surface sexual compulsion seems like a self-inflicted wound, but it's actually an attempt to feel better for things that weren't your fault. Unfortunately, your survival strategy backfires as toxic shame escalates, prompting even more out-of-control sexual behavior.

Dr. Brown says that healing necessitates shame resiliency. For example, secret affairs or excessive porn consumption result in toxic shame, right? If you find relief by processing these events with trusted confidants, sustainable sobriety is more likely. If you don't, the activity will always feel heavy and shameful, leaving you at risk for further acting out. Keep in mind that shame resiliency reduces the likelihood of compulsive sex because it encourages you to set boundaries and limits, which in turn leads to self-acceptance, self-compassion, and self-respect.

The twelve-step slogan "compare and despair" suggests that contrasting yourself to others is another form of shame. You've probably heard the expression "keeping up with the Joneses"—the desire to be as successful as a neighbor in regards to housing, cars, clothing, and the like. Where I grew up, a suburb of Philadelphia, the popular kids wore Lacoste polo shirts that were recognizable by the alligator logo on the chest. My family didn't spend much money on clothes, so Lacoste was not an option for me. As a result, I felt jealous, alienated, and resentful that there was no alligator on my shirt. This sounds silly in retrospect, but I wanted to fit in that badly. In the end I never was part of the popular crowd.

Here are the shame messages many of us absorbed as kids:

- *Am I wearing the right clothes?*
- *How come they live in a bigger house?*
- *My parents drive old cars. Wouldn't I look cooler in a new one?*
- *Why do I go to public school instead of private school?*
- *Wouldn't I be more attractive if I had blonde hair and blue eyes?*

Because shame starts early, it takes lots of disentangling and perseverance to undo the older, more ingrained messages instilled by family, society, popular media, and culture. Do you ever really get rid of them? Not entirely, but you can learn to respond to the shame messages differently. They don't have to haunt you forever.

Whenever you fall into a "shoulda, woulda, coulda" mentality, it's likely due to shame. Each one takes you away from the present and into a fantasy of how events might have turned out differently in the past, resulting in a brighter future. Language is powerful, so I encourage you to listen to how you use your words and reflect on whether they serve you or not. Checking in with yourself and monitoring your use of shame-based words is an act of self-compassion. By limiting language that takes you into the past or future, you'll be practicing mindfulness, focusing on the present in nonjudgmental terms.

The Peculiarities of Perfectionism

Shame is closely intertwined with perfectionism, a form of suffering that grows when you long for something you can never quite achieve. As a recovering perfectionist, I know first-hand how debilitating this critical sensibility can be. Recovery is your opportunity to work on self-acceptance by letting go of unrealistic expectations.

Perfectionism and shame are caused by envy, a toxic feeling that creates more wounding. Envy is an internal shame based on something outside of you and your experience, rather than what's really accessible and happening in your life. This may sound like a stretch, but you actually have everything you need already. It's time to fully accept yourself at any given moment.

The fact is, self-acceptance and perfectionism cannot co-exist. As a kid, I wanted to be perfect in every way. Now I realize that was my attempt to cope with the intergenerational shame pervasive in my family. I didn't understand the notion of imperfection, and always looked outside of myself for approval. As an adult, the twelve-step slogan "progress, not perfection" has been my mantra of imperfection. A majority of sex addicts suffer from perfectionism. What follows here are several versions of the epidemic, and their consequences.

Unreachable Goals: If a goal is not achieved perfectly, it's seen as a complete failure. A perfectionist's standards are unrealistic. Take small steps to achieve larger goals.

The Results-Oriented Mindset: Perfectionists focus too much on the goal and not enough on the process. Learn to be curious about the journey rather than the destination. There will be some stumbling and fumbling along the way, but if you hang on, you'll find comfort and healing in the imperfection of the process.

Defensiveness: Because imperfection is so excruciating, perfectionists react fiercely to constructive criticism. Listen to others with an open mind and heart. Try to find the nuggets of truth, and recognize when people are just trying to help.

Black and White Thinking: Everything is great or terrible. This rigid way of thinking doesn't allow for the flexibility necessary to adapt to the gray areas of recovery. Life is lived on a spectrum of experiences and feelings, not in binary "either-or" outcomes, so pay attention to when you get stuck in the extremes.

Self-Criticism: Perfectionists are hard on themselves and others, which distances them from loved ones. Learn to accept your shame, envy, and perfectionism as temporary states of mind. Be compassionate to your wounded inner child.

Procrastination: Most perfectionists stall. The fear of failure often makes them feel stuck, or too intimidated to get started. Procrastination is fine in moderation, but if you're finding yourself stuck for too long, you're letting shame and self-criticism stifle you. Ask for help from a therapist, coach, or sponsor.

Low Self-Esteem: Perfectionists often go through life unhappy and profoundly lonely as they push others away for fear that they aren't worthy of love. Talk about your low self-esteem with professionals or in twelve-step meetings. In acknowledging your struggles with others, you'll break out of the isolation and create true connections.

Do you have perfectionist tendencies, and if so, how do you deal with them or take contrary action?

Seth: *I still beat myself up at times for certain behaviors, or for not doing things the way I'd like to. But I'm more self-compassionate and self-accepting, and I'm willing to laugh at myself more now.*

Colin: *I can't manage on my own. I need to share them with trusted others in the program, and then look at what the contrary action will be. For me, perfectionism causes procrastination. The contrary act would be something like "what can I start working on imperfectly just to get the ball rolling?"*

Robert: *I've learned to look at the positive side of perfectionism, which is that I like to do things right or have things done a certain way. Everything doesn't have to be 100 percent perfect, sometimes 90 percent or 80 percent is good enough.*

Alex: *I'm a huge perfectionist. I can recall moments where I never felt like my recovery was clean enough. I would talk* *to my sponsor about it and he'd help me see that I tend to be that way with everything. I want to be perfect, and that rigidity is addictive. It's "all-or-nothing" thinking.*

As a lifelong recovering perfectionist, I know how painful it is to live up to self-imposed, unrealistic standards. Not only was my facade of perfection impossible to sustain, my shame held me hostage, isolating me from others, which caused yet more shame, a vicious cycle that continued until I found healing through therapy and the program. Over time I learned how to accept myself, warts and all, but self-acceptance is a lifelong practice. As Pia Mellody says, we are all "perfectly imperfect."

How do you accept your imperfections?

Colin: *To the best of my ability, I try to have compassion. When I'm going into a perfectionistic territory. I take a look at what's going on underneath…usually it's fear, and I try not to be too hard on myself.*

Mario: *Well, I'm still under the delusion that if I try hard, I might get perfect one of these days. It's a daily practice to accept myself the way I am, but there's still the delusion.*

Alex: *I try not to dwell on it or punish myself if I am imperfect. I think that was a big thing for me before. The thing that's working for me right now is saying, "Oh, wow, here I am doing that again." Just admitting it.*

Robert: *Allowing myself to be human.*

Perfectionism is like a wall you built to protect yourself from suffering—usually from childhood wounds. It serves a temporary purpose, but ultimately creates more distance and, in turn, profound loneliness. For me, extreme perfectionism was a way to survive, but eventually I hit bottom and it no longer worked. The pain of perfectionism became way bigger than what it had to offer.

Case Study Three: My Perfectionism

I don't remember when it began because I can't recall a time when perfectionism *wasn't* a part of my childhood. My closet had to be in perfect order. I would hang all my shirts on hangers, including t-shirts, and would never leave a shirt unfolded or stuffed into a drawer. My toys were always lined up against the wall, never left on the floor. My hair had to be combed with a perfect part. A friend of mine would call me Ken, as in *Ken and Barbie*, because it was such a requirement of mine.

In second grade I was assigned a project involving an egg carton, but because my teacher had a thick Israeli accent, I didn't understand it, and instead of asking for help, I cried all night long. What can I say: I was a proud, rule-bound kid. Monopoly was one of my favorite games, but I must have been an obnoxious opponent because I would enforce the rules like a parole officer.

These examples illustrate the suffering I struggled to manage inside myself. My perfectionism had to do with fear and control; fear from living in a turbulent home with three older brothers who felt a million miles away from me emotionally, and with adversarial parents who were chronically unhappy. It was a scary place to grow up—unpredictable, mean-spirited, and volatile. From the time I was a little kid, my home felt out of my control, so I looked for certain things that *were* controllable.

For instance, at age five I inherited my own bedroom, and for some reason my parents allowed us to lock our doors, so when a fight would break out, I would go to my room, slam the door, and lock it. Somehow behind this door I felt safely away from the chaos. This was my attempt to control an otherwise out-of-control situation.

Time moved on, and I evolved from a childhood perfectionist to a perfectionistic adult. In retrospect, I believe that compulsive sex originated from a disowned, rebellious, messy part of me. In some ways, acting out sexually was an attempt to deal with overwhelming feelings of anger, grief, and hurt. But it was ineffective most of the time.

With the help of some talented therapists, as well as the Twelve Steps and very patient friends, I've learned to give myself a break and laugh at myself more. I now know that I can ask for help, especially when perfectionism is debilitating. Knowing I'm not alone has been a great comfort for me. Accepting my imperfection has evolved into a constant practice. The humility to know that I don't have all the answers, and don't have to have them, helps me avoid debilitating shame and self-judgment.

What a relief it is to know that we are all imperfect beings, and that perfection is in fact a myth. Ironically, as a psychotherapist, I've taken on an imperfect calling. I've come to believe that I'm a good enough therapist (sometimes maybe even more than good enough) and remain curious and openhearted. Self-acceptance and self-compassion allow me to stay out of shame and perfectionism more often than not. My perfectionism will never go away entirely, but it doesn't have to block my progress or launch me back into my old obsessive-compulsive ways. With many years now of persistent work, it's a part of who I am rather than my defining characteristic.

Acknowledging your vulnerability is the first step toward deeper connection with others, but perfectionists work really hard to hide their true selves. Shame, envy, and secrecy have been major parts of your sexual compulsion, so you have to apply even more effort, often with the help of professionals, twelve-step programs, and loved ones. It's absolutely possible to show your vulnerable side, and as a result, connection, love, and worthiness will grow. Brown's research shows that it's necessary to have honest conversations about your imperfections in order to develop deeper connection with others and to alleviate shame.

In this anonymous poem, excellence is beautifully contrasted with perfection:

Excellence

Perfection is being right.
    Excellence is willing to be wrong.
Perfection brings fear.

Excellence encourages risk.

Perfection leads to anger and frustration.

Excellence generates power.

Perfection is being in control.

Excellence is being spontaneous.

Perfection is judgment.

Excellence is acceptance.

Perfection is taking.

Excellence is giving.

Perfection is doubt.

Excellence is letting it flow.

Perfection is destination.

Excellence is journey.

Practicing excellence will lead you away from perfectionism and into self-acceptance.

Another dangerous tentacle of shame is judgment. Of course, judgment is a part of life. Every moment of every day we're judging ourselves, others, and the world as a whole. This serves a purpose. It helps you decide how close to get to someone, for example. There's nothing wrong with judgment until it distances you from *all* others or becomes a primary way of relating to the world and your role in it.

Become more aware of your judgmental tendencies, and you'll begin to see how they lead you to avoid intimacy. For instance, this morning I approached a homeless person while walking my dog down the street. I had choices—I could look away as I passed right by, silently judging him. Or I could say hello and acknowledge him as a part of my community. I could also silently send him a prayer of hope. Nowadays I lean into less judgmental choices, but all of these possibilities crossed my mind. In other words, it's not the judgment inside of you that counts—it's how you act in response to those judgments.

At any given moment, I choose to believe others are doing the best they can. Learning to fully accept yourself and the people you encounter this way will bring you peace. Don't get me wrong: there isn't a perfect recovery from perfectionism—because we're all imperfect. This very dilemma reminds us that *imperfection* is human nature. That's not only okay; it's a part of the deal. Practicing imperfection sounds ironic, but on the contrary, it offers a more authentic human experience.

How does this circle back to shame? If you remain judgmental and don't tackle your shame, it will only grow. Your compulsion will continue to have fuel. On the flip side, transparency, sharing, and acceptance help you build shame resiliency.

Shame Resiliency

Learn how shame lives inside you, as well as your shame patterns. It's a complicated emotion, but therapy and twelve-step work are fertile grounds to identify and heal these wounds. Read books about shame resiliency, too, and start a conversation about shame with confidants. By breaking out of isolation, you'll take some of the power away from the shame and move toward more vulnerability and connection.

Group therapy provides another powerful venue for sharing your story. Every one of my group members through the years has let me know that they feel less alone in the world because of it. As Dr. Brown says, "We receive shame from others and we heal shame through others." A therapy group focusing on intimacy and relationships that meets consistently provides an opportunity to re-parent your inner child as well as heal shame.

Obviously, find a sponsor or therapist who is dependable—don't settle for less. Establish new habits to stay in contact with others on a consistent basis and develop a cohesive story about your relationship to shame. These efforts will allow you to let go of the lifelong weight of its baggage.

The language of shame can also be liberating. Begin to use the word "shame" to claim the emotion as a part of you. It doesn't define you. It's simply a part of who you are.

Shame resiliency is a fundamental part of recovery. Name at least one way you've been resilient to shame?

Robert: *My way of coping with shame has been to talk about the things I find so very shameful…to bring them to light and weather it. This can take different forms. It can be through writing a shame inventory where I don't actually have to share it with another person, but it still becomes clear to me. It may just be by sharing with my Higher Power. Ultimately, I find the most benefit when I talk about my shame with someone in strict confidence. I heal through all of that.*

Colin: *The biggest thing is not being too hard on myself. While it's still important to be honest and accountable, I'll say, yes, I'm imperfect, but here's how I'm doing the best I can in my recovery today.*

Seth: *Shame is still one of the things I struggle with. I've done a lot of work around it, and it still feels profound in me. The resiliency doesn't feel like it's there. I'm not sure why. I think I'm better than I used to be, but it's still one of my stumbling blocks.*

Receiving love and compassion is a healing force, but also one of the greatest challenges of long-term intimacy and shame resiliency. By revisiting nurturing experiences from your past, you'll find soothing memories necessary to counterbalance shame and perfectionism. My grandmother stepped into my life during the most turbulent part of my childhood and was a life coach ahead of her time. She believed in me even when I had trouble believing in myself. At the time, it wasn't always easy for me to recognize the depth of her patience, gentleness, and compassion, but that spirit has traveled with me through the years, and the warm, fuzzy memories continue to fill my heart.

If you can't identify an emotionally reliable person in your past, the road to trusting others is more complex. I encourage you to notice moments when you feel more relaxed with people because this is a sign of trust building. It's not that you'll necessarily find these people right away, but if you remain open to the possibility, you'll eventually find such individuals, one relationship at a time.

Reducing your shame also decreases your vulnerability to relapse, since unprocessed shame takes you out of emotional sobriety and creates a slippery slope back to self-destructive behavior. My grandmother showed me unconditional love through cooking my favorite soups, croquettes, and Eastern European cookies, as well as effusively expressing her love for me. I was fortunate that she lived close enough for me to ride my bicycle to her apartment. We would have sleepovers on a regular basis—my place for both emotional and nutritional nourishment. She provided an emotional cushion that prevented me from sinking deeper into my own shame and perfectionism. This is not to say shame wasn't there, but her love and belief in me helped me stay buoyant.

Whatever support was or was not available to you in the past, how you approach love today will determine your healing in recovery. Out-of-control sexual behaviors have likely blocked you from receiving love in recent years, but that doesn't mean love isn't around you. Take inventory of the love available to you now and in the past.

As a therapist, coach, and twelve-step sponsor, I try to believe in others even when they don't believe in themselves. Shame cycles take you into dark places, and it's a tricky path to the light, a trail that requires effort toward more secure attachments than existed before. This takes time and patience.

Shame also manifests as a fear of abandonment. When forging new relationships, you may think: *if they really knew me, would they sprint in the opposite direction?* For intimacy to take shape, we have to let others get to know the real us. This is quite a bind. On the one hand, deep down you've always wanted to be close to others, it just always became sexualized. Emotional transparency requires gradually revealing yourself, one bit at a time.

Instead of beating yourself up for the problematic sexual behaviors of your past, take the opportunity to get to know your imperfections and see what lessons they hold. My mentors taught me how to laugh at my perfectionism and take myself less seriously. As Buddhists have shown for thousands of years, outward compassion and self-compassion are key to contented existence. Learn to be kinder and gentler to yourself, a re-parenting process that requires patience and flexibility.

As discussed in Chapter Two, there are layers of loss that go along with your past actions. Grieving these losses one by one allows you to be more accepting of yourself and establish deeper contact with others. Most of you get along with others in the world, but deeper contact is terrifying. By fully being yourself—warts and all—you'll plant seeds toward meaningful connection.

Because of the shame and secrecy, your sexually compulsive behavior distanced you from others, and in turn you avoided vulnerability. By taking emotional risks and pursuing wise friends, you'll foster meaningful connection. People appreciate honesty, and we're all inclined to sympathize with individuals who express sources of embarrassment and emotional hardship. This will lead to more intimacy in your relationships. By practicing vulnerability you'll share more of yourself, and others will have a chance to finally get to know the real you. This may be intimidating, but it's the foundation to more satisfying relationships. Lean into the love around you and you'll build the capacity to hold more love in your heart, both for yourself and others.

Turning down the volume on shame, perfectionism, and envy is not a solitary process. Sometimes it takes one person to show you the way; other times it takes a group of trusted healers.

Who inspired you to let go of your perfectionism and shame?

Susan: *My sponsor. I tried to pick people who are about ten years older than me because they'd been through it. They always had the best advice and suggestions, and they could see it with fresh eyes.*

Seth: *I worked with a therapist who reminded me of the profound changes I had made. She suggested I do my best to let things go because you can't do anything to change the past.*

Colin: *Fellow members in the recovery rooms…people I see doing the hard work and reaping the benefits, who I admire and respect.*

Alex: *My best friend has been really influential. She's like a sister. I don't trust a lot of people, but I trust her. With her I share everything, and there's this sense of love and compassion. I never feel judged by her.*

As your resiliency to shame grows, you'll finally direct energy toward neglected passions and pursuits. Developing greater purpose turns down the volume on the shame. Ask yourself these big-ticket questions:

- What is my heart's desire?
- What matters the most in my recovery?
- What gives my life meaning?
- What is my reason for getting out of bed in the morning?

Action Steps:

1. Shame is a universal emotion that can be both helpful and destructive. Keep a shame inventory to distinguish between healthier shame and toxic shame.
2. The kid inside you is looking for guidance and healing. Write a letter to your inner child asking what he or she needs from you at this stage of your recovery. Share the letter with your therapist, coach, or sponsor.
3. Shame is here to stay—it's part of being human. Track experiences when you feel more resilient to shame by describing them in a journal.
4. Perfectionism perpetuates shame, and shame perpetuates isolation. Notice current examples of perfectionism and identify what purpose they might serve.
5. Judgment is a form of distancing. Ask yourself what you're protecting yourself from and what you would like to do differently the next time.

Chapter Four

Beyond Narcissism

*No one has probably helped me more
with my narcissism than my dog.*
—Tucker Max

Compulsive sex is an all-consuming, tunnel-vision activity. Nothing around you seems to matter anymore, and there is very little room for anyone or anything else. Self-absorption has taken over. It's an exercise in narcissism.

By contrast, dogs live in the present and focus on others. They are truly one of the best role models of intimacy and unconditional love—loyal, reliable creatures with an abundant generosity of spirit. But dogs also require discipline, exercise, and affection, and this can be your formula to practice *other-centeredness* instead of self-centeredness.

Self-Centeredness vs. Other-Centeredness

Of course, it's okay to be selfish at times. Many of us were told as kids not to be selfish, but in recovery it's essential to strike a balance between our self-care and giving back to others. Occasionally, your recovery from compulsive sex requires a self-centered point of view in order to do deeper healing, balanced with attention toward others as you learn to share more of your true self.

When I was seven years old, my family adopted a four-month-old Siberian husky named Nikki. This was back in the early 1970s. My family was not very emotionally expressive, so Nikki was the receiver of the love we didn't know how to share with each other. He became a focal point of the home as my family moved beyond self-centeredness and poured pent-up affection into this little love machine. On some level, I believe we really did love one another; we simply lacked the tools to know *how* to love one another. Nikki acted as our intimacy instructor for a seminar on love.

More recently, another terrific teacher came into my life, a cocker spaniel named Cooper, and once again a pet demonstrated the power of love through his instinctive desire to give and receive. If you've had a dog, you know their love doesn't compare to anything else. The needs of pets are fairly simple, yet deeply profound, and one core feature is unconditional love and acceptance. If they sense love around them, they thrive. If not, they feel brokenhearted, just like humans.

Pets show us how to give and receive love unconditionally, yet human relationships are much more complicated. For example, people get upset when told something honest that they don't want to hear. They can hold grudges. Humans are unpredictable. Dogs, on the other hand, are consistently loving and eager to spend time with you.

When you lean into love, developing one tender experience and relationship at a time, you discover that it's an essential component to heal from narcissism. But what does narcissism have to do with sex addiction? When you're consumed by sexual obsessions, you unintentionally build a narcissistic bubble—an attempt to feel better at all costs, while avoiding real contact with others. Immediate gratification becomes your sole focus, without any consideration for its effect on others. Since sex addiction involves seduction, fantasy, and intrigue, it provides a powerful rush of admiration and acknowledgment. This temporary state of specialness acts like a drug, eventually requiring more and more adrenaline to satisfy the craving.

Sexual compulsion has been described as narcissistic by nature. Do you still experience yourself as self-centered at times, and if so, how?

Susan: *It's a battle to not be "me, me, me." But when I get into that self-centered place, I become miserable. Nowadays I try to keep myself out of self-absorption and selfishness.*

Seth: *I sometimes turn a conversation around and make it about me when it isn't, bringing attention to myself rather than what the actual issue is.*

Mario: *It goes back to the perfectionism. I'm self-absorbed in the sense that I think I'm responsible for the weather, or an earthquake, or drought. It's negative narcissism—not that I'm the best person in the world but that I'm the worst.*

Robert: *I fall back into a sense of entitlement or feeling victimized.*

Narcissism is known for traits such as self-centeredness and grandiosity, as if the world revolves around you. But these characteristics do not capture the depth of clinical narcissism, which is not only emotionally debilitating, but also results in profound loneliness. The irony is that most narcissists are out of touch with their emotions, so they have trouble accessing their pain. Criteria for a full-blown diagnosis of Narcissistic Personality Disorder, according to the *Diagnostic and Statistical Manual of Mental Disorders,* is as follows:

1. Having an exaggerated sense of self-importance
2. Expecting to be recognized as superior even without achievements that warrant it
3. Exaggerating your achievements and talents
4. Being preoccupied with fantasies about success, power, brilliance, beauty, or the perfect mate
5. Believing that you are superior and can only be understood by or associate with equally special people
6. Requiring constant admiration
7. Having a sense of entitlement

8. Expecting special favors and unquestioning compliance with your expectations
9. Taking advantage of others to get what you want
10. Having an inability or unwillingness to recognize the needs and feelings of others
11. Being envious of others and believing others envy you
12. Behaving in an arrogant or haughty manner

When most of these characteristics are present, the narcissist struggles to establish intimate relationships, or any meaningful relationships at all. These are self-protective qualities that backfire and result in extreme isolation.

Narcissistic qualities exist in all addictive, compulsive individuals. At first, these traits guard you against people getting too close and potentially hurting you. Yet they eventually outlast their purpose, leaving you longing for some kind of connection in your life. This is the most explicit parallel between sexual addiction and narcissism: Hitting bottom is excruciatingly painful, but it also provides an opportunity to recognize your longing for real contact, perhaps for the first time.

If you're humble enough to discover your weaknesses, there's a better chance you'll enjoy sustainable recovery. Many years of specialized therapy along with twelve-step work will often be most effective. An official diagnosis of Narcissistic Personality Disorder only reaches an estimated one percent of the general population, but in my practice, many more struggle with these traits, most commonly the feelings of entitlement, envy, rage, and lack of empathy. Narcissism is a type of suffering that often reveals itself in times of crisis, such as when a person hits bottom with out-of-control sexual behavior.

Because narcissistic qualities are universal, they will also show up in your recovery at times, especially when you feel a need to protect yourself. This is a good thing. It's that alarm clock reminding you to be more self-aware of these tendencies. During an active phase of sexual compulsion, though, these characteristics often reveal themselves in the following ways:

- Preoccupation with fantasies of success, power, or the perfect mate: *your obsessive search for a partner who reflects your specialness.*
- Requiring constant admiration*: your need to be seen, heard, understood, respected, and valued in just the right way at just the right time.*
- Having a sense of entitlement: *an insatiable hunger and belief that you deserve what you want when you want it, similar to a toddler who demands immediate gratification and throws tantrums when denied.*
- Taking advantage of others to get what you want: *lack of empathy for anybody else, as if the world revolves around you and your needs.*
- Unwillingness to recognize the needs and feelings of others: *lack of empathy or guilt.*

In becoming aware of these shortcomings, you will take the first step toward real connection. Through therapy, coaching, and twelve-step work, you'll be liberated from these unconscious patterns. Freedom from your narcissistic qualities requires a desire and a commitment to gradually develop mutually satisfying, intimate connections—but again, one relationship at a time.

We all act entitled to some degree. This can be a good thing if you use it for self-advocacy or assertiveness. Unfortunately, it often becomes something more adversarial. For instance, a client of mine used to rage at all baristas—an easy target since service industry employees are obliged to satisfy their customers. He had an enormous sense of self-importance resulting in expectations for special treatment, so he was always on the offensive, constantly ready to demean any barista who wasn't immediately obedient to his every demand. He took out his misplaced stress, rage, and entitlement on these unsuspecting people. Needless to say, he eventually ran out of places in town to get a morning coffee.

Envy is another destructive narcissistic tendency that comes from a primitive, fragile part of you. Wanting what someone else has is all about comparisons. It's closely related to shame, in that you don't feel good enough, smart enough, or cool enough when envy is stoked. In twelve-step rooms you're warned not to compare yourself to others; too much comparison gets in the way of emotional sobriety. As you explore your narcissism fully, you'll have the opportunity to address your envy, which is not fun, but necessary. It pulls you away from what's really going on inside you. Narcissistic envy fuels judgment and separates you from people you perceive to be more or less successful than you.

Judgment also serves a vital purpose. We're still animals with survival instincts, and judgment is our internal barometer to know when we feel safe or threatened. Use your best judgment to identify your people—the ones you can count on—and don't invest in those who are undependable. Judgment allows you to find your tribe. In your everyday life you make countless judgments; when you sense your narcissism surfacing through grandiosity, arrogance, or self-centeredness, recognize it as an indication of deep-seated insecurity or shame. By diagnosing your own behavior this way, true belonging will replace the isolation you've known so well.

Just as compulsive sex is rooted in brokenheartedness, your narcissism was a way of dealing with that pain. Although it helped you dodge thoughts and feelings that caused suffering, eventually the strategy quit working and became downright destructive. But as much as your narcissism acted as a distancing pattern, the wounds can now pave the way toward closeness. Learning to lean on reliable people, you'll slowly build trust and safety, with toxic judgment, entitlement, and envy diminishing over time. Consider the case of my client Bill.

Case Study Four: Bill's Narcissism

Bill isn't a full-blown narcissist, but he struggles with an extreme version of self-centeredness and insensitivity. As a child, he always needed to be right, and acted like the world revolved around him. His well-intentioned parents poured everything into their children at the expense of their own dreams, each working two jobs to provide their kids the advantages they themselves had lacked. With great opportunities, however, came extreme pressure to succeed. Bill embraced the high expectations, and as the youngest child, with a genius IQ, he felt extra special and believed he deserved to be treated as such.

At school, Bill excelled. Teachers told him he had the potential to go far. At home he was the hero child, treated by his parents as the eventual key to relieving them from financial hardship. The excitement only grew as he got older and announced his goal to become a doctor. But instead of feeling grateful for his parents' sacrifices, he became obsessed with adoration. As a teenager, he used masturbation as a stress-reliever, and then started to expose himself and masturbate in public places like libraries and cars to add adrenaline to the experience.

When Bill started to have sex with women, he focused solely on his orgasms. He lacked emotional connection to his partners and found relationships tedious. In college he learned about escorts and "happy ending" massage parlors, where he enjoyed a feeling of complete control and minimal emotional contact. These non-relational sexual experiences fit his narcissistic personality. After Bill finished his dermatology residency in his late twenties, he had more free time, which he devoted to sexual conquests. Although his problematic sex life had been compartmentalized before as a recreational activity, it soon became all consuming.

In his early thirties, Bill met Janet, who fell in love with him in spite of his attempts to push her away. He knew Janet was a catch, but still felt like an ill-equipped teenager. She saw beyond his achievements and felt like there was more to Bill than he would let on. He was curious and terrified by love at the same time. Until then, he had never felt warm, loving feelings toward a potential mate, and never imagined someone would be so patient. After dating for close to a year, Janet was getting worn down by his attempts to keep her away. She wasn't going to hang around much longer if he didn't get help. This was Bill's version of "hitting bottom."

After Janet's ultimatum he started therapy, and was in turn recommended to a twelve-step group for sex addiction. Reluctantly, he attended all of his appointments and meetings, and little by little, his heart and nervous system thawed. Bill learned that his rage originated from the expectations and pressure he felt as a child with parents who wanted him to rescue them. Sexual acting out became his way of discharging rage, and his attempts to maintain distance from Janet were a way to avoid being hurt. Underneath every narcissistic exterior is a fear of intimacy, and it worked for Bill for many years, until Janet broke through his wall.

"Now I see my blind spots," he says. "They've been there since the beginning. It's been a lonely road and I have a long way to go, but I hold out hope that I can be closer to Janet as I learn how to put myself in her shoes."

Bill and Janet are still struggling but attend couples therapy consistently, as well as a local meeting of Recovering Couples Anonymous. He is willing to do whatever it takes to work on his patterns of entitlement, self-absorption, and envy. Janet is skeptical but open to the possibility of their relationship taking shape and moving forward in a gradual way. As Bill creates points of emotional connection, his capacity for other-centeredness expands, and his narcissistic tendencies will hopefully continue to fade into the background.

The Healthy Side of Narcissism

Although narcissism is generally seen as a negative trait, *healthy narcissism* is critical to child development. It's how your confidence and self-esteem take shape. According to Freud and other psychoanalysts, all children possess a sense of omnipotence and grandiosity as they enter the world, where they strive to receive the gleam in the eye of their caregiver. In recovery, it's essential to find that gleam of appreciation and approval from caring friends and confidants, rather than countless sex partners or people who are emotionally unavailable.

Otto Kernberg and Heinz Kohut, two renowned psychoanalysts, believe pathological narcissism arises from inconsistent childhood interactions that lacked empathy. Freud called these emotional wounds "narcissistic injuries," and they result in a walling off from or lashing out at others. As adults, narcissists lack empathy and as a result maintain few, if any, meaningful intimate relationships. Their childhood wounds also result in narcissistic rage—withdrawal, irritability, and occasionally violent outbursts. They can be expressed outwardly (like at service workers) but often get internalized.

The human need for attunement, mirroring, and connection from birth means that in order to thrive, as infants we need a primary caregiver who has a capacity for unconditional love, empathy, and a here-and-now presence. This is what's referred to as a secure attachment. There are always gaps in that availability, though. So while narcissism originates as a desire for closeness, it evolves into an affliction that causes emotional destruction.

In committed relationships, you might attract partners with codependent tendencies who act selflessly and enjoy taking care of others. As a result, you feel attended to, and your partner feels valued while experiencing a sense of purpose. Since you may use grandiosity, self-centeredness, and arrogance as a protective wall, you are the distancer in the relationship, while your partner falls into the pursuer role. In order to move beyond narcissism, you'll need to pursue your partner more. Ideally, your relationship will become more balanced and satisfying when you lean into the love and initiate intimate moments more often.

The pursuer-distancer roles can change over time, so your partner may need to give you space or provide loving detachment while you learn to lean into the relationship safely and gradually. Sexual compulsion is avoidant, distancing, and narcissistic by nature, so it takes extraordinary patience and perseverance from both parties to balance your roles. The pace may feel glacial at times, but if both of you are truly invested in learning about yourselves and each other, it's possible. By utilizing couples therapy or the twelve-step fellowship of Recovering Couples Anonymous, you'll have support to do this intimate work together.

Being of Service

One of the themes of twelve-step programs is service to others. Why do you suppose that is? It boils down to *other-centeredness*—the ability to get out of your head through a focus on bettering the world. The addictive, compulsive mind is a dangerous place to stay for too long. It grabs your attention, yet recovery requires a willingness to give your mind something else to do.

The lingering effects of narcissism as a tool against suffering, and compulsive sex as a shield against hurt, are powerful. It's essential, then, to feel safe with others in order to lower your defenses. Offering people help is a sure-fire way to get there. This might sound counterintuitive, but initiating contact and stepping toward others is a path to connection artfully described in The Prayer of St. Francis:

The Prayer of St. Francis
Lord, make me an instrument of your peace:
where there is hatred, let me sow love;
where there is injury, pardon;
where there is doubt, faith;
where there is despair, hope;
where there is darkness, light;
where there is sadness, joy;

O Divine Master, grant that I may not so much seek
to be consoled as to console,
to be understood as to understand,
to be loved as to love.
For it is in giving that we receive,
it is in pardoning that we are pardoned,
and it is in dying that we are born to eternal life.

Although I was raised in a liberal Jewish home, this prayer's message always resonated with me. It's often used in religious and non-religious marriage ceremonies. Feel free to modify it in a way that works for you. And regardless of your spiritual or cultural background, I urge you to consider how this prayer illuminates other-centeredness and generosity.

If you aspire to live a life of serenity, hold the intention for love in your heart at all times. This awareness will support your well-being if practiced on a consistent basis. When you move beyond your obsessive mind and put yourself in other people's shoes, empathy expands, while self-centeredness dissolves. As a result, your innate generosity of spirit reveals itself and becomes a habit of the heart. These spiritual principles may seem foreign to you, but they are practiced throughout the world. If this particular prayer doesn't work for you, find your own affirmations or mantras that are more in alignment with your recovery.

On a practical level, there are plenty of ways to be of service both in and outside twelve-step rooms. All of your relationships, both personal and professional, are opportunities for other-centeredness. For instance, I have interns in my practice who teach me all the time about humility, innocence, and curiosity. I do my best to offer them the same nurturing support that was given to me when I first started out.

In 1992, after finishing graduate school, I was invited to join a group private practice under the wings of two very talented and generous therapists. I was in my late twenties and still near the beginning of my own recovery and healing journey. Not only were they patient and understanding of my youthful limitations, they also challenged me to be the best new therapist I could be. They raised me as a professional at a time when I needed strong, loving parenting—a secure attachment, if you will. Nowadays, I get to give back what I was given, as a living testament to the St. Francis Prayer. Once you focus outwardly, chances are you'll attract love in all areas of your life.

In recovery, it's often suggested that you be of service to others. Describe how that has worked for you.

Alex: *I sponsored a lot of people in twelve-step programs. They would call me daily and we'd talk about the steps and what's going on in their life. I also do things in meetings like secretary, literature, coffee. In the community I do free HIV testing. And I do community outreach events as part of my school.*

Robert: *I brought a twelve-step retreat that was very important to me in the U.S. to the German-speaking twelve-step community.*

Colin: *Taking others through the steps and being available to
              pass on what was given to me. I can also be of service by
              practicing the principles in all areas of my life, in whatever
              situation I'm in, whether it's work, family, friends, or a
              relationship, and even out in the world at the grocery store.*
Seth: *I've given workshops. Showing up at meetings I almost
              always share, and I think that's being of service.*

Being of service is a surefire way to have meaningful contact with
others. Because narcissism is profoundly lonely, it requires courage to
break out of the isolation and create real connection. Imagine a castle
with a piranha-filled moat and a closed drawbridge blocking visitors.
Your narcissism built this fortress with a clear purpose—to keep out
intruders who might be a threat. Isn't it time to take the risk and open
your heart to others?

A painful dilemma ensues when you finally long for true connection,
yet fear letting others in. Most sex addicts suffer from this tension—
desiring closeness but not knowing how to move safely toward it. Your
narcissistic wounds have caused isolation and withdrawal, and if you
continue to manage these uncomfortable feelings with compulsive
sex, you will perpetuate your obsessive-compulsive tendencies. True
connection is the remedy, no matter how risky it seems.

If you have been living life barred off from emotional expression,
it's time to take a leap of faith and lean into the love that awaits you.
It's there. Now is the time to find it. It's painfully clear how narcissism
interferes with intimate relationships and intimacy, but how do you
move safely toward others if you're used to being holed up in your castle?

**Do you find that you have trusting relationships? If so, what
helped you build greater trust?**
Seth: *The real key was to be with somebody honest and truthful
              who I could rely on. Deception drives me crazy—lack of
              honesty is really tough.*
Colin: *Taking the time to get to know somebody to make sure
              they're a trustworthy person and then also looking out when*

challenges come up in the relationship. How the other
person responds, and how the negotiation process goes, and
if the other party is willing to work on that, or is at least
mindful of where they overstepped, is very important.

Mario: *In the recovery rooms I met people I felt I could trust*
because we shared the same shame, imperfections, and
secrets. There was no risk of being betrayed, because there
was nothing to hide.

Susan: *I think the biggest thing is just to go slow.*

In Sex and Love Addicts Anonymous, many people identify as *love avoidants* or *love anorexics*. When I first heard the term "anorexic" in the context of sex and love addiction, I didn't quite grasp the kind of deprivation experienced by these overwhelmingly lonely people. It turns out *all* narcissists are emotional anorexics when it comes to intimacy. Real love involves mutual respect and trust, an utterly terrifying prospect that requires patience and perseverance.

Leaning into Love

Trust takes shape over time with a person you can truly count on. But if your trust muscles were not strengthened as a child, it will take endurance to build them as an adult. Many years may be needed, even if you're willing to be faithful to the process. Find your people—those who are steadfast supporters and also want to travel this trust journey with you. By investing in yourself, you're already on the road to more meaningful intimacy and in turn less likelihood of relapse.

Do you have a confidant? How did you develop this relationship?

Alex: *I have a handful of people that I tell everything. I really*
say it like it is. I'm not going to bullshit them. They're like
my God Squad.

Robert: *I do have a few people I feel very close to. I can talk to them*
about almost anything. I've developed these relationships

> *through the work in the twelve-step fellowship. Showing up, being honest and sharing what's really going on, and also admitting when I made a mistake.*
>
> **Mario:** *My sponsor was the first person I had no secrets from. By learning not to have secrets and trusting that he wasn't going to reject me, I learned how to be honest with other people in my life.*
>
> **Seth:** *I have a dear friend—not program-related—who I just always felt safe with. Feeling safe, not judged, and that the information would be kept in strictest confidence, that's a special thing.*

Warning

As I said before, engaging more deeply with others is a wise idea, but it's okay to be cautious. Relationships are complex and unpredictable, and moving beyond self-centeredness and into other-centeredness can be disappointing. Occasionally you'll let down other people. At times your friends and family will disappoint you. This is inevitable. Dealing with those frustrations or disillusionments is how you'll grow.

Carl Rogers, a founding father of humanistic psychology, coined the terms *unconditional love* and *unconditional positive regard*. Ideally, you at least got a taste of these experiences as a child, but most of you probably felt a gap between the love and attention you desired and the distractible, anxious, depressed, and narcissistic behavior your parents actually expressed. Your desire for love faces the task of bridging this intimacy gap with your relationships today. Fortunately, thanks to neuroplasticity, you *can* learn new behaviors over time despite your well-worn habits. With determination and tenacity, it's possible to move from isolation to intimacy.

You're reading this book, so you already have the mindset, and possibly the *heart-set*, to seek help and consider a more fulfilling future. It shows enormous courage and humility to embark upon the road to intimacy. Just remember that you're not alone. Others have shown the way, and you can carve out brand new neural pathways as you navigate beyond narcissism and into the world of meaningful, sustainable connection.

Action Steps:

1. Dogs are role models of unconditional love and acceptance. If you have a dog, be mindful of your relationship with your beloved pet and notice moments of deep connection. If not, foster a pet to learn from this unique love instructor.

2. Lean into the love around you. Take stock of your relationships and make a list of emotionally reliable individuals in your life (or those you would like to depend on more). Also keep a gratitude list of all sources of love in your life.

3. Narcissism is part of being human. Acknowledge the healthy narcissism within you and take stock of times when you feel confident and comfortable in your skin, while also recognizing occasions when narcissism distances you from others.

4. Entitlement, envy, and judgment are traits that both protect and distance you from others. Track examples of these coping strategies as a way to build awareness of these patterns.

5. When you were sexually compulsive, your generosity went dormant. Make a daily list of your other-centered activities, no matter how small. This paradigm shift moves you out of your own head and into the world. Consider the following:

    a. What do I have to offer others?
    b. How would I like to contribute to my community?
    c. How can I make a difference in the world?

6. Loving relationships are built one person at a time, and the more trustworthy connections you cultivate, the more solid your recovery will feel. Improve existing relationships by giving more of yourself. Be a dependable friend to others without expectation.

Chapter Five

The Rhythm Within

*It's not a magic ride, yet there are still moments that
feel magical. Coming from my desert, finding my oasis,
yet not always knowing what to do when I get there.*
—Burt Schaffner

What does it really mean to be in the moment? You mindfully notice the present, for one. You get in deeper contact with yourself and others in the here and now—with your mind, body, and spirit—rather than dwelling on the past or worrying about the future. It takes courage. When you were sexually compulsive, you lived your life outside of yourself as you attempted to escape your emotions.

Spending more time in the present requires you to feel all of your feelings. Ideally, the past offers sentimental value and lessons learned, and the future suggests new possibilities, but it's in the present where you'll experience a deeper connection with yourself and others. For example, having lunch with a friend can either be a superficial experience or a chance to talk honestly about what's really going on inside you. How many times have you felt empty after time with a close friend? How often do you feel more nourished, because you chose to share more of yourself, and also listen? Emotional and sexual sobriety are more attainable and sustainable when you practice genuine contact with those you trust.

Painful feelings will always pass. Sometimes they will stall, sometimes they will barely crawl, but eventually they move along. A wise twelve-step slogan says, "This too shall pass." In this chapter you'll learn how to build capacity for the present when you feel ready to let go of avoidance, denial, and compartmentalization.

Slowing Down

When you were sexually compulsive, it was always about seeking the adrenaline rush of sexual conquests. In recovery, it's about being in the here and now, living mindfully, taking deep breaths, and cultivating relaxation. Although sexual escapades once allowed you to regulate your nervous system and feel good in the moment, over time compulsive sex dysregulated your nervous system and took you further away from feeling like yourself. Compulsive sex was un-grounding, whereas recovery provides the opportunity to feel grounded and more like yourself more of the time.

After I finished graduate school in the early 1990s, I joined a consultation group led by an innovative psychologist named Burt Schaffner. Not only did he share a multifaceted version of human development and personal growth, Burt also helped me take myself less seriously. We only understand ourselves fully if we slow down and listen to "the rhythm within," he said.

Busy-ness was a wall that blocked me from being attuned to my inner experience—my everyday feelings, thoughts, and sensations. It protected me from vulnerability and prevented me from taking risks in relationships, resulting in loneliness even when there appeared to be plenty of loving people in my life. Through the years, I've learned to slow down through meditation, yoga, simple breathing exercises, and journaling. As a result, my awareness of the rhythm within has grown exponentially. Burt's powerful words always stay with me because he described what all sex addicts experience. And this is my intention—to help you recognize your unique *rhythm within*.

When you slow down and listen closely to your inner world, you discover parts of yourself that have been missing in action—feelings, sensations, wants, and desires, to name just a few. It takes practice and discipline to cultivate mindful awareness, and initially it may be quite uncomfortable for you. You've muted what's really going on inside you for so long, you've become accustomed to avoiding your true self.

Do you take the time to slow down and have downtime in your life today?

Seth: *It's much better than it used to be. I used to be the Energizer Bunny and couldn't take time to relax...I think that was part of my addiction. If I wasn't acting out sexually, I had a lot of compulsive busy-ness. In recovery I sit down more often with a book or I get a cup of coffee or play my guitar, just hang out or sit still for a little while. I'm much better at that.*

Colin: *For me, that means daily meditation, ten minutes in the morning, twenty minutes in the evening, creating space for breaks throughout my day so it's not one activity after another, which can run me down.*

Robert: *In the morning I take time for myself...a short meditation, a yoga stretch, and time for my coffee, and then my day works better.*

Susan: *Another pattern I had was to run until I dropped. I used to go out from 5 a.m. to midnight, six days a week. On the seventh day, I couldn't move. It felt like a truck had run over me. Now I try not to schedule every minute of my day and I do a lot better. I can sit and watch my favorite TV shows for an hour or two... I can just chill out.*

Susan illustrates what psychoanalysts refer to as "manic defenses," what Seth describes as his addiction to busy-ness. Defenses always protect us from something—in this case, pain. If you keep yourself distracted by tasks, you're trying to avoid something. Slowing down and listening more deliberately to yourself is a courageous attempt to safely and gradually let down your manic defenses as you begin to savor the slower, more satisfying possibilities around you. Whenever you feel triggered, see if it's possible to wait five minutes. At the end of five minutes, notice how you feel, and take note of any shift.

In the throes of out-of-control sexual behaviors, you experience constant cravings and engage in compulsive efforts to feed these cravings, to try to feel better, or to feel less. Paying attention to your internal world as well as your surroundings is an art—imprecise, and hardly something you're capable of doing overnight. It's a creative process that takes time, patience, and inner exploration. In America, *doing* is the accepted norm, and if you don't have an overscheduled life, there must be something wrong with you. Yet recovery offers you a healthier option—*doing* in moderation. Slowing down in the midst of your manic defenses. Walking rather than running. Stillness and mindful action in lieu of frenetic activity.

Once the sexual hunt is over, then what? Being on the prowl for sex, love, and validation provided excitement and pseudo-aliveness, but no sustainable satisfaction. It became a time-filling distraction. And it never met your ultimate purpose—to feel vitality, connectedness, and deeper love. So how does slowing down make room for these more fulfilling experiences?

It begins with reclaiming what's inside of you, which is only possible through emotional sobriety. Yet here is the painful truth: just because you slow down and listen more carefully to your rhythm within doesn't mean your inner experiences will be warm and fuzzy. If anything, it's likely to be the opposite. Your suppressed emotions—anger, sadness, hurt, joy, fear, guilt, shame, love—will surface unpredictably and haphazardly. This creates turbulence, because you haven't experienced this part of you since before the sexual compulsion began. Getting reacquainted with the waves of your emotions may be stressful, but that's how you create new neural pathways. At times, it may feel as though you're drowning in emotion, so make sure you have a life raft available—a therapist or a sponsor who can be with you in moments of trouble.

Stress and anxiety are inseparable, but here is what makes each one distinct. Stress is your response to a perceived demand. A friend asks you to help him move, and you don't want to disappoint him, but you don't have the time or energy. This triggers stress.

Anxiety, on the other hand, manifests in your thoughts, emotions, and behaviors. It's a worry or nervousness about an uncertain potential outcome. For example: imagining a hurtful interaction with an ex-partner should you run into each other at the coffee shop. In the twelve-step community, anxiety is often referred to as "future tripping," and with my clients I call it "catastrophizing." Either way, it's an agonized focus on a future you feel is out of your control.

Stress can come in response to positive or negative experiences. Try not to categorize your emotions that way, though, because all emotions are a valid part of you. For our purposes, *distress* is an unpleasant response to an undesirable event, such as losing a job. *Eustress*, as well as the term *stress*, was coined by Hans Selye, a Hungarian endocrinologist. He refers to eustress as a physiological response to a desirable occasion, such as a wedding. Because stress is a natural reaction to life's experiences, it's a necessary component to your recovery too. Without stress, we would all be lifeless blobs of protoplasm. Everything in life can be a source of stress, so dealing with it safely and productively is a daily practice.

In the past, you may have acted out sexually before, during, and after stressful events, but what are your options now? There are limitless choices to take contrary action and they all require commitment, discipline, and accountability. For instance, you feel stressed out because your mother is hosting a family reunion and you haven't seen many of these relatives in years. What are your options? You can choose to attend. You can tell your mother you can't make it. You can limit your participation to an hour or two. You can bring a friend for moral support. Remember that you're never locked into anything; you get to choose which solution feels right for you and your recovery. Let's look at another case in which someone found a recovery plan that lifted her out of sexual addiction.

Case Study Five: Linda's Rhythm Within

Linda went to her first twelve-step retreat for sex addiction more than twenty years ago, when she was thirty-five. At that time, she didn't know what to expect. All she knew was that she wanted to get out of her hometown to slow down and work on the steps. Since then, she has been to more than twenty retreats and considers it a staple of her recovery.

"I grew up an only child in the 1970s near Boston," Linda says. "My dad tried his best to be a good father, but he traveled all the time, and my mom was hooked on benzos. I wanted a parent to pay attention to me, but they were never around, and my anxiety and loneliness grew."

Linda suffered from a severe case of father hunger, which led her to gravitate toward boys from a young age. She saw girls as mean-spirited and competitive, so she kept her distance from them. Besides, they loved to gossip about her letting older boys have sex with her.

In her twenties, Linda was having sex with every guy she found attractive. It started out rather innocently when she realized as an older teen that men would give her the attention she craved, and she soaked it up. Over time, it grew from innocent flirtation to constant intrigue and obsession. Eventually, it turned into regular one-night stands, phone sex, and compulsive masturbation.

Sex became a sport for Linda, and she could teach a course in the art of seduction. At the same time, it felt increasingly less satisfying. Linda wanted to stop, but couldn't. Her neighborhood clinic knew her by name, because she contracted STDs regularly. Linda was terrified she might get HIV. She heard about a twelve-step program from her counselor at the clinic and decided to give it a try.

In her first meeting, she immediately felt at home. Linda found a sponsor, started working the steps, and attended her first retreat. It was a revelation.

"As soon as I arrived at the retreat house near San Diego, my body felt calm and peaceful," she recalls. "My unquiet mind had a chance to slow down and take in the love of the fellowship and the nature all around me."

Having grown up in New England, Linda felt like an outsider in California. She moved to Los Angeles for college and always felt out of step there, but knew intuitively that finding a way to relax would be necessary to sustain her recovery. The retreats have been a sanctuary to slow down and help other women in the program relax as well.

Since then, Linda has been a faithful part of the twelve-step community and has found many ways to relax, including deep breathing, swimming, and of course retreats. She sometimes finds herself thinking compulsively about her self-care activities, but acknowledges that it's a far healthier way of life.

And while she never gravitated to formal meditation, Linda takes moments throughout the day to acknowledge her mind-body-spirit connection. She also abstains from looking at her phone until after breakfast. At first this was not easy, but now she enjoys this boundary as part of her quiet time. After waking up, she reads a page from *Answers in the Heart*, a daily meditations book, and does a ritual of morning stretches to establish contact with her body. Linda then mindfully sips a cup of tea in her garden and silently acknowledges her gratitude for the day. Although her morning tone-setter does not include traditional meditation, it has a meditative tone.

"Establishing some kind of constant contact with a power greater than myself is the foundation for the rest of my day," she says. "Now I get to cherish my time to slow down and listen to the wisdom inside and around me."

Stress Relief Strategies

Dr. Selye said, "It's not stress that kills us, it is our reaction to it." Addictive, compulsive behaviors are often triggered by intolerable stress reactions—a feeling, thought, or sensation that is too much to endure. For example, you get in an argument with your girlfriend. Instead of connecting with a confidant and talking it out, you make a beeline to your computer and get lost in pornography. When you engage in problematic sexual behavior in response to stress, it only postpones the stored feelings. The challenge instead is to slow down and try to respond in a more regulated, self-nurturing way. When you overreact to life's stressors, you create more stress for yourself. Emotional sobriety requires you to observe yourself, make deliberate choices, and choose sober actions with each and every stressful situation.

Stress is unavoidable, but if you respond to it productively, you minimize the amount of distress that goes along with it. Just like recovery from sexual compulsion, stress relief is about harm reduction and lowering the possibility of stress-related disease. Choose a more productive and compassionate approach to coping with stressful events. You don't have to carry your stress alone—ask for help when you need it. There is no right or wrong way to go about this, only an opportunity to navigate stress more effectively.

In graduate school I was part of a research team that investigated how middle-school teenagers in Los Angeles coped with stress. Kids tend to be our best teachers if we listen to them, and one of our primary findings reminded us that, as Dr. Selye said, it's not the stressor itself, it's how you perceive and respond to it. For instance, all of the teenagers in the study described moderate to heavy academic stress, but only some seemed to suffer as a result. What was the distinguishing variable? The kids who had meaningful and supportive relationships fared much better than those who felt isolated. This is a simple reminder that asking for help from an effective support network can minimize the effects of stress.

Share your stress with a trusted confidant. Ask for a hug and a listening ear. There are as many ways to respond to stress as there are stressors, but few strategies are as effective as airing your thoughts and feelings to a supportive person. It makes you feel comforted and understood, diminishing the potential toxic effects of stress.

What do you do to cope with stress?

Seth: *Exercise. I hike a few times a week and that helps, especially when I'm feeling uptight. I work things out in therapy...I process things. I talk to a friend. Sometimes I'll just stop and breathe. I've had limited success with meditation, but I try to do that sometimes, even on my hikes.*

Colin: *I use the tools (of the twelve-step program). I pause, check in with my Higher Power, make an outreach call (to a* *friend in the program). I say a prayer, slow things down, and just remind myself, "No big deal."*

Susan: *Long brisk walks. A really intense yoga class really helps me and I do so much better if I have daily meditation. Also, singing helps. Chanting. Eating three healthy meals a day.*

Alex: *I exercise. Today I ran a few miles, which really gets my head clear and makes me calmer. Insight meditation is really important for structure. Even if it's just fifteen minutes, it's a remarkable difference in my way of thinking.*

Robert: *Things that used to stress me a great deal that I felt were very important, I realize are perhaps not as important as I thought, and I allow myself to re-focus and put things in perspective.*

The teenagers from the Los Angeles research project showed how much dependable people can impact your personal well-being and help you manage stress more effectively. The same goes for stress related to out-of-control sexual behaviors. Surrounding yourself with reliable people increases your chances for sustainable sobriety. When your trust in a person is validated, anxiety diminishes, and you feel regulated by the contact with them. When the opposite occurs, your stress will stay the same or increase over time. It's as simple as that.

This principle also applies to emotional and sexual sobriety. If you're white-knuckling it all the time in isolation, recovery is going to be more slippery for you. It's about surrounding yourself with like-minded people who also want to get better, but it's also about finding the right people—not those who simply sit around and bitch and moan. There is nothing wrong with commiseration, but I recommend you do it in moderation.

You control your emotional state—the outside world does not. We can be miserable and blame everything on others, or we can change our mind. Many of you can relate to the notion that life dealt you a bad hand, and it's probably true to some extent, but how you play your cards matters just as much, if not more. Learn to manage your rhythm within through exercises such as meditation, therapy, or chatting over a cup of coffee with a friend. You can safely open up an inner world that was shut down during your sexual compulsion days.

Many of my clients say things like "he made me angry" as they unintentionally blame others. I always correct their word choice. Nobody can *make* you angry; something inside you was triggered, resulting in *your* anger. You are not a puppet.

When you're triggered, something from your past is activated. You may not be able to identify it, but usually you'll go into fight, flight, or freeze mode, a reminder that something old has surfaced. For instance, your father calls you selfish because you choose not to attend a family function, so you feel emotions similar to when he called you selfish as a kid. Because of this put-down, you feel shame and end up shutting down. But instead of withdrawing or reacting aggressively to the perceived attack, you can choose to take care of yourself in some of the following ways:

- Mindfulness strategies
- Deep breathing
- Building resiliency and buoyancy
- Contacting a confidant
- Expressing yourself clearly, directly, and honestly

When triggered, take the opportunity to empower yourself rather than act the victim. Remember, you're not responsible for other people's feelings, and other people are not responsible for yours. Disappointing people is inevitable, and being disappointed by others is too. Hurting and getting hurt is also part of the deal. Being triggered feels like having salt poured into an old wound, yet it teaches you about parts of yourself you didn't know existed. These blind spots are growth opportunities if you pay attention to what they are communicating.

Here are a few specific grounding rituals for when you experience conflict:

- Visualize the person as happy (if necessary, use a photo).
- Ask yourself: *What is it I find most annoying? What quality of theirs do I like the least?*

- Locate that quality somewhere in yourself. They are your mirror.
- Ask your Higher or Universal Power for the willingness to do what is necessary to change your attitude.
- Regarding the other person, repeat over and over: *Teach me to love him/her exactly the way they are in this moment.*

It's an emotional paradigm shift when you realize you have an internal locus of control and your inner world is up to you. People often seek therapy when they feel like something external has rocked their internal world. This exercise is a way to help change your inner experience regardless of the crisis. There's no getting away from stress, but how you face it can be the difference between staying sober or not.

Again, it's not about distracting yourself from stress and anxiety; that would be like a psychological and spiritual bypass. It's about identifying the stressor, building perspective, and coming back to the here and now as efficiently as possible. Being in the present is a practice, and here is a list of healing options to remind you that there are many ways to combat stress and anxiety. Employing even just a few of these strategies will help you find relief and move toward emotional sobriety:

- Individual psychotherapy
- Group psychotherapy
- Physical exercise
- Nutritional balance, only using caffeine, sugar, and alcohol in moderation
- Consistent sleep habits
- Yoga
- Meditation
- Deep breathing
- Somatic Experiencing and Brainspotting
- Learning the physiological mechanics of anxiety
- Reading books and articles related to anxiety relief
- Practicing imperfection
- Practicing gratitude
- Exploring spirituality (or whatever gives your life meaning)

- Cultivating humor and laughter
- Creating downtime daily / scheduling time off
- Unplugging from technology
- Volunteering / being of service
- Music: listening, playing, singing
- Developing nurturing self-talk ("I'll do the best I can for today")
- Therapeutic massage / somatic bodywork
- Pet therapy
- Progressive relaxation / visualization / guided imagery
- Build self-awareness and track anxiety triggers
- Practicing self-acceptance and self-compassion
- Homeopathic / Ayurvedic / naturopathic medicine / psychopharmacology

The Art of Relaxation

Meditation is a time-tested anti-anxiety strategy that dates back thousands of years. My story with it is like that of many others who have given it a try. For many years, I dabbled in various approaches to meditation, but for whatever reason it never turned into a consistent practice. After many failed attempts, I finally decided to take a more structured approach. I enrolled in a Mindfulness-Based Stress Reduction (MBSR) class, which met every Sunday night for eight weeks.

This time it stuck. Maybe I was finally ready to integrate meditation into my life. Maybe the financial investment in the course was the catalyst for me to get the best bang for my buck. Maybe the structure, accountability, and mentoring made the difference. It's always about timing, and in my case it required the commitment of enrolling in a class.

What I learned and continue to learn is that meditation is one of the best anti-anxiety medications on the market, and it doesn't even require a prescription. When your anxiety is down, your emotional sobriety is up, so I encourage you to experiment with meditation of any kind—whatever resonates is the version that's right for you.

There's no right or wrong way to go about it. Nobody will scrutinize your meditation practice. Try to have fun and leave your perfectionism at the door. As I continue to refine my morning ritual, I find that it's an essential tone-setter for my day. Each morning I stumble toward my cushion (sometimes in the dark or early dawn), and my dog Bowie follows me into my meditation corner. It's become an intimate ritual—not always easy or peaceful—but a space we've carved out just for us. As a matter of fact, when I begin to meditate, I always notice restlessness in my mind and body, and I've come to understand that part of the process is to settle down and be patient with myself. An absolute blank mind is not realistic, but coming back to your breath and achieving moments of a quieter mind is still therapeutic. As a recovering perfectionist, I find it's another priceless exercise in imperfection.

As to the specific meditative practice, there are limitless ways to develop and sustain the routine. It requires some trial and error. Here is my version of a morning tone-setter:

- Sit quietly on a cushion in a designated space in your home. It can be any time of day, but try to find a consistent time if possible.
- Read a page or two from an inspirational book, a meaningful prayer, or an affirmation that resonates with you.
- Sit quietly for ten to fifteen minutes. When your mind wanders, keep coming back to your breath. Don't focus too much on the amount of time you meditate. Start slowly and increase it over time.
- Congratulate yourself for your commitment to a morning ritual and express gratitude for your healing space.

Don't be rigid with these suggested steps. Do what works best for you and know that it will require patience as well as discipline. Now that I wake up fifteen minutes earlier each day to meditate, I do lose a bit of sleep. But it's worth it to me because I've set a positive tone, and the rest of my day seems to go smoother as a result.

Most of us are familiar with the classic image of the Buddha sitting cross-legged with closed eyes. This position may or may not work for you. You may find that sitting on a cushion or a chair with proper back support feels better. Running, swimming, and walking can also be meditative movements. Don't confine yourself to meditating at home in the wee hours of the morning, either. Experiment and find your natural rhythm.

Dr. Jon Kabat-Zinn, psychologist and founding Executive Director of the Center for Mindfulness at the University of Massachusetts Medical School, has shown that mindfulness meditation regulates the nervous system and helps you build resiliency and buoyancy—a powerful rival for stress and anxiety.

Our culture encourages us to achieve our goals as quickly as possible, so allowing a process to unfold at its own pace can feel revolutionary. Mindfulness also allows you to get to know yourself more fully. It's one thing to understand these concepts on an intellectual level, but it's another thing to put them into practice.

Sex addiction is often about living in the extremes. How do you pace yourself and find moderation in your life today?

Alex: *I used to believe that you didn't have a good workout unless you were really sweating and panting and felt like you were going to vomit. I don't do that anymore. If I can be more flexible with myself, that works a lot better for me. It's not so much about extremes or rigidity.*

Colin: *The biggest thing to help with moderation is having my routine and structures in place. Doing daily outreach calls and prayer and meditation every day.*

Mario: *Mostly accepting when people point out that I still need to rely on other people. Before, I would say, "Oh, no, no, no…you don't understand, this is the way I'm supposed to do it. If you don't like it, go away." Now it's like, "Oh, yes, you're right. I'm sorry. You're right."*

Mindful Recovery

Mindfulness has taken the world by storm these past few decades. Its roots are thousands of years old, yet when I refer to mindfulness meditation, I'm referring to the work of Dr. Kabat-Zinn, who originally studied chronic pain patients in a hospital setting. Upon developing a structured course in mindfulness skills, he found that patients who participated in the program reported fewer pain symptoms. Since the 1980s, his methods have taken the meditation world to new heights, helping people from all walks of life.

At its core, mindfulness is simply an awareness of the present moment done by your "observing self." A portable practice, it can be done while walking the dog or washing the dishes. It's a way of being that requires repetition because, as neuropsychologist Dr. Donald O. Hebb once said, "Neurons that fire together, wire together," meaning that the more you practice something, the more your brain recognizes it as habit. The choice is yours. Do you continue down the well-worn path of destructive behaviors, or do you practice safe and purposeful ways of engaging with life? Mindfulness also encourages you to remain curious, compassionate, and grateful—all elements of a sustainable recovery.

Sexual compulsion and fantasy take you away from the here and now, but mindfulness puts your mind back into the present tense. Addiction is full of blind spots—innocent-seeming actions or feelings that lead to relapse—and mindfulness is a mirror to reveal those blind spots and make you keenly aware of your everyday choices. The following poem describes this evolution from blind spots to clarity.

Autobiography in Five Short Chapters
by Portia Nelson

I
I walk down the street.
There is a deep hole in the sidewalk.
I fall in.
I am lost... I am helpless.
It isn't my fault.
It takes forever to find a way out.

II

I walk down the same street.

There is a deep hole in the sidewalk.

I pretend I don't see it.

I fall in again.

I can't believe I am in this same place.

But it isn't my fault.

It still takes a long time to get out.

III

I walk down the same street.

There is a deep hole in the sidewalk.

I see it there.

I still fall in.... it's a habit... but,

My eyes are open.

I know where I am.

It is my fault.

I get out immediately.

IV

I walk down the same street.

There is a deep hole in the sidewalk.

I walk around it.

V

I walk down another street.

Mindfulness gives you options. The choice to keep your eyes open. Through this awareness, you can take responsibility for your addictive past and not fall into the hole in the sidewalk repeatedly. It's empowering to know that you don't have to relapse over and over again.

When I worked as a hospice social worker, I sometimes felt unsure what to say or do with patients who were facing death. In Chapter Two, I mentioned the wise chaplain who told me it's not about the specific words or actions you choose, it's your ministry of presence that matters most. Simple, yet profound. And you too can be of service to others by listening to them with an open heart and mind. When you're truly able to live in the moment, mindfulness can also be like providing this ministry of presence to yourself.

I encourage you to investigate the abundance of possibilities that go along with getting to know what's inside you. Drop into yourself for a moment as you finish this chapter, and see what resonated for you and what didn't. What resonates the most will serve as a clue for further exploration as you get to know the rhythm within.

Action Steps:
1. It's easy to forget that you're a human being, not a human doing. Take a few minutes each morning to slow down and listen to what's inside you. Create a morning tone-setter through meditation, journaling, or inspirational reading.
2. Compulsive behaviors create stress, anxiety, and drama. As you choose to practice emotional sobriety, learn to navigate the stress and anxiety more effectively through emotionally reliable relationships.
3. Mindfulness comes in many shapes and forms. Choose one form of mindful awareness, such as savoring your favorite food or listening attentively to your favorite music.
4. The ministry of presence is the gift you give to others by simply being with them in the here and now. Choose someone in your life, and mindfully share yourself freely.
5. Living a life of moderation requires mindfulness. Take note of when you are thinking and living in the extremes, and track choices you make toward moderation.
6. Meditation is one of your greatest allies. If you're open to giving meditation a try, take a class, go on a retreat, or find a local sitting group. If you already practice, challenge yourself to create more time for this self-care practice.

Chapter Six

Regulating the Nervous System

Trauma is not what happens to us, but what we hold inside in the absence of an empathetic witness.
—Peter Levine

When I attended graduate school in the early '90s, there was no mention of the nervous system in my classes. The mind-body-spirit connection may have been a brief footnote, but all I learned about the nervous system was the fight-or-flight response, a survival instinct mentioned in undergraduate psychology classes. In the few decades since then, most curriculums have adapted to not only include the nervous system, but also emphasize its tremendous influence on how we heal.

While addictive, compulsive behaviors can help you feel better, the relief is short lived, as the suffering always returns. Sexual compulsivity hijacks your brain, resulting in chronic nervous system dysregulation, perpetuating the turmoil inside you. Dysregulation is a disruption of your autonomic nervous system—an up-regulation that can cause panic attacks or rage, or a down-regulation that may lead to dissociation or disconnection. Either way, there's an imbalance, leaving you with one of the greatest challenges in sexual recovery—reclaiming regulation and resiliency.

Regulation and Dysregulation

Dr. Peter A. Levine, the founder of Somatic Experiencing and author of *Waking the Tiger*, believes that it's essential to restore the wisdom of the nervous system, which in turns rebuilds your vitality. The nervous system is your internal temperature gauge, letting you know when you need heating or cooling to return to resiliency and resourcefulness. You're more likely to relapse when dysregulated, and to stay sober when regulated.

One strategy to move from dysregulation to regulation is through *resourcing*: recalling memories of love and nurturing to calm your nervous system. For instance, if you have a memory of playing with your dog in the park on a beautiful spring day, reimagining that scene will help you regulate. With practice, resources can become the touchstone of your nervous-system health and leave you less vulnerable to use sex as a mood regulator.

Other "brain-body therapies" that help regulate the nervous system include Somatic Experiencing and Brainspotting, which involve tracking your physiological sensations, grounding yourself in your body, and reorienting toward a balanced nervous system without the use of compulsive sex. We've long known that "the body remembers"; trauma gets shelved in the subcortex of the brain, a storage place for highly unpleasant memories and experiences that were too much to process at the time. Stored trauma may come out in ways that are clear, such as rage and terror, and ways that are subtle, like vague sadness, irritability, or shutting down. When you understand more about the brain-body connection, you're more equipped to handle compulsive cravings, and as a result see that relief is within reach.

So what exactly does the nervous system have to do with sexual compulsion? Our bodies have instinctive functions, like breathing, blood circulation, digestion, elimination, and sexual arousal. These are managed by a nervous system that is divided into two parts—the sympathetic and parasympathetic branches; the sympathetic branch registers when to fight, flee, or freeze, and the parasympathetic system focuses on resting and digesting. When the nervous system becomes over-activated or under-activated, all of your basic functions are impacted, leaving you challenged to return to equilibrium. For example, your daughter's teacher calls to let you know she's crying uncontrollably from being bullied on the playground and wants to go home. Immediately, your heart rate increases. You feel warm and flushed. The nervous system has propelled you to drop what you're doing and pick up your daughter right away. But if you're a sex addict, your nervous system may respond differently.

After hearing about his child's distress, the sexually compulsive father gets anxious, which automatically takes him to thoughts of acting out sexually. Although these sexual fantasies have been meant to temporarily regulate his nervous system and cope with his anxiety in the past, in this case, it serves as a form of avoidance from a serious situation rather than a productive way to cope. Hopefully, he finds a way to pick up his daughter, but initially his brain was hijacked from the task at hand.

When you feel highly dysregulated, you look for anything to get out of the emotional pain. If sexual compulsivity has become your go-to behavior to reduce suffering, that's where your mind goes. But eventually the sex addiction progresses as you look for more dangerous, adrenaline-seeking behaviors to escape the pain, and the cycle continues. In order for balance and regulation to become a familiar internal state, you'll need to practice self-regulation daily. This can only occur, though, when you've learned to recognize when you feel most regulated and dysregulated—when you feel more like yourself or not—which may necessitate help from a somatic therapist. The goal is to feel resourceful and buoyant most of the time. Because we live in a world full of addictive temptations, it's a constant challenge to build somatic awareness and to be mindful of what's really going on inside you.

In a regulated state, you experience deeper contact with yourself and others, whereas dysregulation causes isolation and disconnection. Let's look at the example of my client Debbie.

Case Study Six: Debbie's Dysregulated Nervous System

When I first spoke to Debbie on the phone, she said she was losing sleep, but wouldn't say more. When we first met in person, eye contact was minimal and her posture was poor. I've seen this many times. It's almost always related to trauma, shame, and helplessness. During the appointment, Debbie barely looked up to see me, as if she was wondering whether it was safe enough to be herself and share her whole story. She was in her early thirties, and her capacity for real connection had been severely limited.

I reassured her she could say as much or as little as she wanted, and we would get to know her nervous system through feelings, thoughts, sensations, images, and memories. Sometimes words were helpful, but oftentimes slowing down and building somatic awareness in the here and now would be her primary focus.

Over time, Debbie opened up about the challenges she was facing. She disclosed that she used to have sex almost every day, and when she wasn't with a partner she masturbated compulsively, sometimes to the point of self-injury. Currently she struggles with flashbacks and nightmares. She also had acute anxiety, especially in dark places like movie theaters. Little by little, Debbie shared the depth of her brokenheartedness. She was anally penetrated by a male teenage babysitter when she was seven years old, and a gym teacher exposed himself to her multiple times when she was fourteen.

From the time she was old enough to talk, Debbie's parents had told her she was a very beautiful girl. Unfortunately, her mom grew highly envious of her beauty, and was extremely critical, even suggesting she had seduced the boy and the teacher. Instead of feeling protected by her parents, she felt alienated, abandoned, and profoundly misunderstood.

When she hit puberty, Debbie had lots of sexual fantasies of men and women that felt confusing, overwhelming, and overstimulating. Due to the experience with her babysitter, sex terrified and excited her at the same time. She tried to downplay her looks by wearing baggy black clothes, but still received lots of sexual attention from both men and women.

By the time she moved away for college, Debbie was having sex with men and women multiple times a week—sometimes multiple times a day—and it was becoming riskier, involving anonymous sex and public liaisons. On the one hand, the validation felt intoxicating. But at the same time, it left her feeling lonely and hollow. She knew the sex medicated residual pain from her childhood trauma, but her nervous system was getting worn down, resulting in panic attacks, insomnia, and dissociation.

Through therapy, she began to gain awareness of when she felt regulated or dysregulated. This awareness empowered her. She felt hopeful to no longer be at the mercy of her traumatic past. When she found a pleasant memory of a relationship that felt calm and grounding, we'd pause to help her nervous system experience a deeper sense of safety. Discovering both internal and external resources is crucial to sustainable healing. Our therapeutic relationship became one of her resources, both in the office and during the week, as she began to trust that collaboratively we could heal her nervous system.

We also acknowledged that her history of compulsive sex regulated her nervous system temporarily, but only acted as short-term relief for deeper issues.

It's been five years since I first met Debbie. Now, her nightmares and flashbacks are less intrusive, but still show up at times of extreme stress. Her sleeping patterns have normalized. Debbie recently become involved with a man she describes as loving and patient, and she chose to share her background of sexual compulsivity and trauma with him. As a result, she feels closer and more connected. Debbie's willingness to take emotional risks in this relationship builds her capacity for intimacy, and that emotional bond strengthens her nervous system resiliency.

Window of Resiliency

It doesn't matter whether a dysregulated nervous system is the cause or the effect of your sexual compulsivity. In the end an awareness of dysregulation, along with the willingness to practice a more regulated lifestyle, will promote sexual and emotional sobriety. This takes patience, practice, and perseverance. Find a somatically trained professional who fully understands the nervous system, and a missing piece of your sexual recovery puzzle will be revealed.

A regulated state can be called your "window of resiliency" When you get "up-regulated," it feels like the accelerator inside you revving in high gear. This manifests in things like panic attacks or rage. If your nervous system slams the brakes (down-regulation), you can feel disconnected and shut down. Dysregulation is inevitable, and finding your way back to a regulated state is your healing direction each and every time.

Elaine Miller-Karas, LCSW, executive director of the Trauma Resource Institute, a nonprofit that cultivates trauma-informed and resiliency-focused individuals and communities throughout the world, developed the following diagram to illustrate regulation and dysregulation in the nervous system.

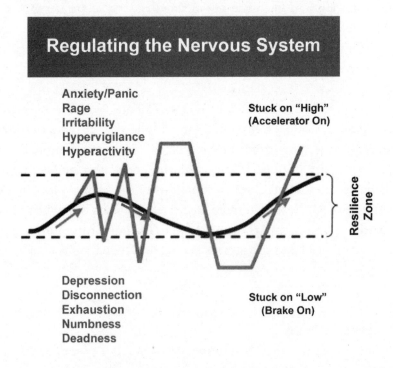

Adapted from Elaine Miller-Karas, LCSW, Trauma Resource Institute

The space between the two dotted lines illustrates when you're feeling most resilient and buoyant. In other words, when you feel most like yourself. When you bump out of the resilience zone due to past trauma or life's stressors, you're vulnerable to feeling stuck on "low" or stuck on "high." Something is too much to process. But it's not the dysregulation that counts—it's how you attend to it.

**Sex addiction often flourishes when pain is too severe to
endure, and compulsive sex is an attempt to regulate that
experience. How do you regulate your emotions without falling
into old patterns?**

Colin: *I try to be present with the feelings, recognize they're there,
and use the tools of the [twelve-step] program to catch the
feelings, pray for healing and support, make an outreach
call, breathe, and get back into my body. When it starts
feeling like it's overwhelming me, I turn my attention
to how I can be of service to somebody else, or what's
something productive I can do to balance the emotional
intensity.*

Alex: *Meditation is the reset button for me. I think a lot of
times I get into a trance of pain or suffering and then I
want to act out, but when I meditate, I see it. I see what
I'm doing, and it's painfully obvious, and it wakes me up
so that I at least have a little more choice in the matter
and know what I'm doing instead of just blindly doing it.*

Seth: *Before, I just couldn't realize it and I would act out. A lot
of times I didn't even know I was feeling difficult feelings.
Now I've learned when I am, and that they will pass, and
that sometimes I just have to acknowledge them. I will
take them to therapy. I may call a friend. I think part of
my process is not to fight it—to just acknowledge it, and
to know it will pass.*

Brain-Body Approaches

Over the last few decades, several new somatic therapies have been
developed and refined, and even more sophisticated approaches to
trauma healing are being fine-tuned all the time. Although there are many
reputable, effective approaches, I focus on the following two brain-body
methods I use in my practice.

Somatic Experiencing (SE)

In Dr. Levine's book, he recalls observing animals in the wild and how impressively they recover from life-threatening situations. Even though they are routinely exposed to potentially traumatic events, they rarely exhibit trauma symptoms. Animals have a resiliency to trauma that we don't. Or at the very least, humans tend to be more *complex* in response to trauma; we find ways to override the animal instinct necessary for quick healing. Somatic Experiencing practitioners believe that trauma symptoms are the effect of a disturbance to the balance of the nervous system, but that humans have an innate capacity to heal when they recalibrate.

The key to understanding why these symptoms occur lies in your body. When you experience trauma, often you're encouraged not to show it—not to shake, tremble, or cry—because of how hard that may be for others to see, or for your own pride. The opportunity to release the trauma impact is missed, and instead these memories and experiences are stored within, eventually resulting in a dysregulated nervous system. On the other hand, if you're fortunate enough to have a loving, nurturing person with you at the time of a trauma, the event may be fully processed then and there. So a tragic event may be traumatizing for some, yet leave others unscathed, depending on their respective support networks during and after the traumatic experience. Your history of trauma will also influence future experiences of highly stressful events, as you'll likely have decided based on previous relationships whether vulnerability can be safely expressed, or should be stifled.

Dr. Levine made another observation of animals in the wild that is relevant. In addition to noting their resiliency to trauma, he observed that when an animal doesn't escape a predator, a different survival instinct kicks in. At the moment of capture, it falls immobile. This instinctual reaction, called the *freeze response*, is a kind of altered state that allows the animal to avoid being eaten by the predator, since animals sometimes become disinterested in their prey if the target is playing dead. But it also has survival value; if the predator doesn't immediately kill its prey, the animal can wake from this trance and escape unharmed.

This freeze state is also key to understanding trauma. Your fight-flight-freeze response needs to come to successful completion for the nervous system to return to a state of equilibrium once consciousness returns. For example, if as a child you were physically abused by a stepfather, you had little recourse at the time but to take it. He would probably have abused you further if you fought back. But somatic therapies help you retroactively express the unexpressed. This may come out as tears, or temperature changes, or as words that were not spoken at the time. When you're unable to complete these responses in the moment, your nervous system goes into a freeze state, and this frozen, immobilized emotional state can look calm on the outside but internally is comparable to what happens in a car when you put your feet down on the brake and accelerator at the same time. A huge amount of energy is throttled usually below conscious awareness, creating symptoms of trauma such as sexual compulsivity. But regulating your nervous system through the completion of stored trauma prevents vulnerability to relapse.

Somatic Experiencing (SE) and Psychotherapy

What does SE look like in the therapeutic relationship? Trauma is part of life. I would guess that all of you have been traumatized somewhere along the way. Although not all traumatic events result in symptoms, physical and behavioral complications due to trauma are epidemic. Unresolved trauma may show up in the following ways:

- Addictive and Compulsive Behaviors
- Anxiety and Panic Attacks
- Rage and Impulse Control Issues
- Depression, Disconnection, or Dissociation
- Chronic Pain
- Migraines
- Gastrointestinal Problems
- Chronic Tension

SE typically takes place in face-to-face sessions and teaches you how to track sensations in your body. It's effective for both *specific trauma* and *developmental trauma*, examples of which are:

Specific Trauma:
- Car Accidents
- Natural Disasters
- Sexual Abuse/Assault
- Physical Abuse
- Domestic Violence
- Catastrophic Injuries
- Surgeries

Developmental Trauma:
- Abandonment
- Neglect
- Loss
- Verbal/Emotional Abuse

There are countless more versions of traumatic events. But Kathy L. Kain, a senior faculty member with the Somatic Experiencing Trauma Institute, provides this clear and simple definition of trauma:
1. Something bad happens.
2. You don't know how to deal with it.
3. It gets stuck inside of you.

If your body knows how to heal, then why hasn't it done so? Just as you have an animalistic part of your brain that focuses on survival responses, you also have higher-brain regime of emotional and cognitive responses, which often interfere with this natural process. In other words, you overthink it. Somatic Experiencing taps your mental awareness to help your body access its innate capacity to heal and resolve trauma.

Brainspotting

In 2003, Dr. David Grand, psychotherapist and founder of Brainspotting, held a session with an aspiring figure skater who couldn't land the triple loop, a jump that would take her skating to the next level. The sixteen-year-old had attended sessions with Dr. Grand for more than a year to receive a treatment called EMDR, or Eye Movement Desensitization and Reprocessing. EMDR practitioners believe that the nervous system processes and resolves trauma through the back and forth movement of the eyes. Then one day Dr. Grand stumbled upon a new healing method.

When allowing the eyes to be fixed on one spot, his client had a tremendous emotional release, as well as eye wobbling and involuntary movements in her body. The client was processing childhood trauma and performance anxiety in a way she had never experienced before. The next day the skater went to the rink and reported to Dr. Grand that she could not miss the jump—instead, she landed it each and every time.

From this point forward, Dr. Grand started to explore the possibility that discovering a "brainspot," a distinct place in the visual field where activation and processing occurs, would lead to deeper processing. His work showed that Brainspotting, as it came to be called, is not only an effective trauma-healing approach, it can also be used to treat other unpleasant or disturbing experiences, such as addictions, grief, anxiety, and creative blocks.

Brain-body methods build somatic awareness and more effective regulation of your nervous system, which can provide a greater capacity to feel more like yourself. Brainspotting and Somatic Experiencing are both cutting-edge methods that combine neurobiological and relational attunement to address a wide range of mental health issues, including out-of-control sexual behaviors and relationship ruptures.

Talk therapy engages the neocortex, your thinking, conscious brain, while somatic therapies access the subcortical system, where you store unresolved trauma. Neuroscientific research shows that painful memories can get stuck in the nonverbal, noncognitive, subcortical brain, which blocks your ability to live fully in the present. Brainspotting harnesses the brain's natural healing process by utilizing the visual field to accelerate healing.

The effectiveness of somatic therapy in regulating the nervous system has led to its worldwide acceptance. In my practice, I introduce these options to all my clients, including those in addiction recovery. Even if they opt primarily for talk therapy, understanding their nervous system can be healing in itself. Bringing together thoughts, feelings, and body awareness offers a multidimensional approach to healing. In the past, I focused primarily on feelings and thoughts with my clients, which was helpful but limited. Somatic approaches help you thaw safely and gradually as you get your brain, body, and spirit back in line. As neuroscience continues to reveal more about the regulation of the nervous system, we will all learn together. "All I know is that I know nothing," Socrates said. It's good to stay humble as we learn together about the restoration of your nervous system, one of the keys to long-term sexual recovery.

Somatic therapy is a wellness and empowerment model—a collaborative, respectful relationship unlike any other. Mutual regulation takes place when the nervous system is positively impacted by a loving or nurturing connection, such as one you may have with a therapist, coach, sponsor, or pet. Think of it as two nervous systems communicating with one another. In the best conditions, secure attachment grows. The relational attunement gives you the rare, safe experience of someone else being with you fully.

There's a more complete list of references toward the back of the book, but here are some of the most popular somatic approaches utilized now by psychotherapists and trauma specialists worldwide:

- Brainspotting
- Somatic Experiencing (SE)
- Trauma Resiliency Model (TRM)
- Eye Movement Desensitization and Reprocessing (EMDR)
- Neuro-Affective Relational Model (NARM)
- Sensorimotor Psychotherapy

Regulating the nervous system is a path back to your true self, and in turn to sustainable sobriety. Although I primarily use SE and Brainspotting in my practice, all of these modalities are worth considering, depending on what's available in your community. As always, be sure to find a somatic therapist who is a good match for you, and who understands addiction recovery too.

Feeling regulated can be described as the time you feel most like yourself. When do you feel most like yourself?

Robert: *I feel more regulated when I'm connected to nature and my Higher Power.*

Colin: *When I'm consistently working my (twelve-step) program, or when I'm with a friend who truly sees me and supports me.*

Alex: *When I've slept at least eight to ten hours, when I'm eating regularly, when I have a connection with God, and when I'm loving myself. If I'm regulated, my clothes are clean, I'm brushing and flossing. I don't feel like I'm reacting so much to other people's nonsense.*

Susan: *When I'm creative—writing, singing, dancing. When I'm doing artwork, and when I do public speaking.*

Seth: *Doing something I really enjoy and being with people I enjoy. Sometimes there is a lighthearted side of me that comes out in those moments when I just feel like me.*

Interpersonal neurobiology, a field of study developed primarily by Daniel J. Siegel, MD, psychiatrist and founding co-director of the Mindful Awareness Research Center at UCLA, focuses on attachment patterns and their effects on the brain. In the past, scientists thought an individual's neurological growth ended by the end of adolescence. But we now know that it continues throughout your life, a perpetual capacity for change referred to as *neuroplasticity*. So you can teach an old dog (or for our purposes, an aging human) new tricks.

Dr. Donald Hebb built off this phenomenon when he said, "Neurons that fire together, wire together." Understanding that your neural pathways connect and expand through practiced, consistent behaviors, you can rebuild and reconnect neurons that promote a healthy internal balance. For instance, if you meditate ten minutes each morning, your brain learns to recognize the experience of slowing down and being still, and applies those skills on other occasions.

As mentioned earlier, another simple regulation tool is *resourcing*. Therapists sometimes use the "safe place" exercise inviting their clients to remember a place that helps them feel calm and peaceful. For example, I attended college in Western Massachusetts and lived in a house next to a farm with horses. I chose to live there in the quiet summer months when school was out of session, and even as I write this, the sights and smells of this peaceful New England setting return to me. As I take a moment to track my nervous system, my breathing slows down, and I find myself smiling inside and feeling more tranquil. This pleasant memory lives inside of me and is accessible at any time. It will always be a resource.

By focusing your attention on pleasurable, life-affirming activities, you can regulate your nervous system. You may already take stock of the gratitude in your life, but think of resourcing as an expanded version of a gratitude list.

So, at any given time, you have a few options related to your nervous system:

1. Stay on autopilot and ignore the cues your nervous system gives you.
2. Remain dysregulated in moments of distress and take a passive approach to feeling better.
3. Get to know your nervous system and live a more buoyant, resilient life.

It doesn't matter how long you've ignored your body's cues, it's possible to carve out new neural pathways. Having your nervous system chronically activated, or triggered, is often due to relational patterns, stories of the past, and old buttons in need of repair. For example, a coworker tells you something you perceive as critical. Whether or not it was intended that way is secondary to the fact that you experience it as criticism. You're triggered into shame, which automatically evolves into an out-of-proportion reaction, leaving you dysregulated. You may up-regulate into rage, or down-regulate into hopelessness. Either way, you suffer a distorted reaction caused by memories of painful experiences with criticism. So how do you work through a trigger?

This is where somatic mindfulness and thoughtful processing can heal old patterns. In twelve-step programs, it's recommended that you pause when agitated. Wise advice, but it takes ongoing practice to bite your tongue, breathe, and wait a moment for the willingness to respond rather than to react. If successful, pausing will prevent escalation and allow you to catch your breath before acting out your feelings. This is also an opportunity to practice grounding, orienting, and resourcing as you return to your window of resiliency. Generally, you know you're there when you do a body scan and the level of activation has subsided.

Over time, you can deconstruct the incident with a somatic therapist, look at your part in the interaction, express the unexpressed feelings, and consider your options for the next time your buttons are pushed. For now, you may consider keeping a log that tracks activating events. Awareness of your reactions is the first step toward healing. Empower yourself by knowing that many alternative responses are possible.

Attachment Patterns

Reliable relationships are what help infants regulate their nervous systems, and attachment patterns are founded in this connection between a baby and its caregiver. Unfortunately, many of you did not have emotionally dependable parents, leaving you at risk for compulsive behaviors.

In 1988, British psychoanalyst John Bowlby wrote *A Secure Base*, which sparked a vital conversation among clinicians and researchers about the bond between an infant and its primary caregiver. Dr. Bowlby developed specific categories for the attachment styles he observed. These styles mainly refer to the child's reaction to separation from its caregiver, perceived threats in the environment, and possible harm of any kind. The conclusion was that if you have a secure attachment with your caregiver, you're able to regulate your nervous system more easily and show more resilience. But if you had an insecure attachment, self-regulation becomes more challenging in childhood, as well as in later life.

Although there are four major categories in the attachment literature, the two most common among sex addicts are Avoidant Attachment and Anxious Attachment. The other two categories are Secure Attachment and Disorganized Attachment. Secure Attachment occurs when there is a *good-enough* parent, and generally speaking, children with addictive, compulsive patterns don't fall into this category. On the opposite side of the spectrum is Disorganized Attachment, which refers to someone who grew up in a highly chaotic and unstable environment and developed little to no capacity for attachment due to an absent primary caregiver.

Babies who grew up in a crowded orphanage would be one example, and those with Disorganized Attachment have a steeper attachment mountain to climb.

Later on, we'll take a close look at the intersection of attachment patterns, love addiction, and love avoidance. But here I want to focus on two attachment patterns in the context of the nervous system.

Avoidant Attachment

When a primary caregiver lacks the capacity to respond effectively to your needs, you experience them as emotionally unreliable. You become counter-dependent and self-sufficient, or "need-less and want-less," as Pia Mellody describes it. The misattuned parent creates a child who likewise denies needing support from others and has an *avoidant attachment*. This is the birthplace of love avoidance (sometimes called intimacy avoidance). Individuals learn to build relational walls to prevent feeling disappointed or overwhelmed.

In its most extreme form this attachment style shows up later as *sexual or emotional anorexia,* a pattern of profound isolation and loneliness. In either case, self-soothing or compulsive sexual behavior may be an attempt to regulate the nervous system. Turning away from mutual regulation with others becomes the survival mechanism of choice because people are seen as emotionally undependable. Chronic masturbation is a prime example of a misguided effort to regulate the nervous system.

Anxious Attachment

When a primary caregiver is responsive and nurturing on some occasions, yet intrusive and insensitive at others, you're left anxious, insecure, and sometimes ambivalent, not knowing which version of the parent will show up at any given moment. You walk on eggshells and become highly distrustful, all the while feeling starved for contact. This type of inconsistent attunement results in an *anxious attachment.*

This is how love addiction and obsessive fantasy originate. In order to regulate the nervous system, the child seeks some type of soothing from the caregiver but never knows when, or if, it will come. As a result, the child is often desperate for contact and love that are only intermittently available.

How does attachment style relate to long-term sexual recovery? As we discussed, you can teach an old dog new tricks, but doing so takes determination and endurance. If you were not raised with a secure attachment, and most of us were not, it's not too late to establish secure attachments as grown-ups. Just because there were attachment gaps in your past doesn't mean you're destined to remain avoidant, ambivalent, or anxious about relationships and love.

Find emotionally dependable relationships that offer you reliable and loving experiences, and they will be your growing, secure base. Be patient with yourself, and notice when your nervous system feels relaxed and calm. If you're feeling more relaxed, your nervous system is letting you know that you're trusting more—a sign that you've found contact you can count on.

When was the last time you felt most like yourself? For me, singing in my car, laughing with friends, and being silly with my dog is when I feel like myself. Ask yourself what makes you feel that way. Which activities allow you to feel comfortable in your own skin? This is another way to measure a regulated nervous system.

Action Steps

Familiarize yourself with this short glossary of nervous system language:

1. *Grounding:* an awareness of your body's physical contact with the ground or something else that stabilizes it such as a supportive chair. Ground yourself anytime you feel dysregulated.

2. *Orienting:* your attention to the environment around you; you notice your surroundings and let your eyes go wherever they want to go. Orient yourself whenever you feel dissociated or disconnected. In *Brainspotting,* Dr. Grand states that "where you look affects how you feel."

3. *Pendulation:* the natural swing in the nervous system between pain or discomfort and sensations that are neutral or pleasant. Pay attention to the natural waves of your nervous system.

4. *Resilience Zone:* When you feel most regulated and more whole in mind, body, and spirit—sometimes called "being in flow." Savor times of resilience by letting yourself take note of these warm, fuzzy, internal experiences.

5. *Resource:* A positive characteristic, a pleasant memory, a person, place, animal, or thing that provides calm and peace. Use resourcing anytime you feel dysregulated and need to ground yourself.

6. *Titration:* Gradual exposure to sensations of distress, discomfort, or pain to prevent overwhelming your nervous system. Be patient and gentle with trauma healing. You always get to choose how much or how little you delve into it.

7. *Tracking sensations:* Pay attention to your physical sensations. By tracking, you'll move away from being a talking head and experience more connection to your brain and your body.

Chapter Seven

Cultivating Contentment

It takes a lot of courage to show your dreams to someone else.
—Erma Bombeck

Brokenheartedness is often the cause and always the effect of sex addiction, leaving you vulnerable to relapse. One of the most essential tasks then for long-term, sustainable recovery is to find ways to fill the emptiness inside you. Of course, it's not realistic to expect a nourishing and fulfilling life right away. First, you need to be curious about the possibility of vitality expanding inside of you.

Positive Psychology can help. With a focus on human strengths and virtues rather than deficits and pathology, it counterbalances the heaviness of the disease model of addiction. Its practitioners ask questions regarding personal engagement and purpose, such as, *What gives your life meaning? When do you find yourself flourishing? And how would you like to be remembered?* Great possibilities lie ahead if you slow down enough to do careful soul-searching. Your heartbreak will continue to mend as you develop a more purposeful roadmap based on what matters most to you.

In early recovery it's often challenging to identify what brings you joy. Because there tends to be so much emphasis on pain and suffering, the idea of past flourishing often gets overlooked. Yet finding moments of contentment and serenity in your past is crucial. Maybe those times were few and far between, or maybe they are lost and forgotten, but together we'll excavate these missing memories.

Think first about your core values. They take shape in childhood and become more deeply held beliefs over time. For example, your sixth grade teacher asked you to give a presentation about a social cause with which you identified. You researched the number of animals euthanized in the U.S. each year, and spoke passionately about the need for more protections. As a result, your core value of animal rights was further etched inside of you. As you identify these values, you clarify your highest priorities, such as contribution, community, and accomplishment. By declaring what matters to you, you'll find new purpose and momentum.

Positive Psychology, sometimes called "the science of happiness," has demonstrated the life-changing impact of positive emotions and character strengths, tools often neglected in addiction recovery programs. Dr. Martin E.P. Seligman, a distinguished psychologist, pioneered research on *learned helplessness* and *learned optimism* and the effects these traits have on well-being. Eventually serving as the Director of the University of Pennsylvania Positive Psychology Center, Dr. Seligman is considered the founder of Positive Psychology, which embraces strengths-based, wellness-oriented approaches to mental health.

This paradigm shift was nonpathologizing, meaning it doesn't focus on what's wrong, but rather on what's right. This may seem rather logical, but at the time it turned the world of psychology upside down. Historically, sex addiction has been categorized within the disease model, pathologizing compulsive sex. Now, in line with Positive Psychology, a wider range of viewpoints are opening up, with a focus on such things as sexual health and the role of attachment styles. As a sex addict in recovery, you will fall into patterns of self-shaming and self-attacking, and Positive Psychology proposes the opposite focus—leveraging strengths, examining gratitude, and exploring forgiveness.

In the Twelve Steps there is a necessary emphasis on resentments and character defects, which helps you understand the triggers that led to your addiction or may cause relapse. But working the steps is only part of the healing process. To counterbalance the heaviness of the steps, give equal attention to your character assets to reinforce the positive aspects of who you are. Making room for pleasant experiences will regulate your nervous system and teach your neurons that there's more to life than the burden of suffering.

Positive Psychology is not meant to replace the traditional roots of psychology, but instead complement existing approaches for better overall mental health. Clarifying your values and identifying personal strengths will help buffer you against relapse.

When Dr. Patrick Carnes introduced the term *sexual addiction* to the recovery community in the early 1980s, he also presented a powerful treatment model that adapted elements of the twelve-step program crafted by Alcoholics Anonymous. He saw a parallel between sex addiction and the disease-based model of drug and alcohol recovery. Instead of "compulsive sexual behavior" or "out-of-control sexual behavior," "sex addiction" became the mainstream term for this behavior. Unfortunately, this label also carries shame, stigma, and misunderstanding. When people hear that an individual is receiving treatment for sex addiction, they assume something is terribly wrong with that person. The affliction is seen as a mark of weakness. On the contrary, acknowledging the problem and seeking help requires strength and courage, and through recovery one embraces what's right in their life—the desire to mend their broken heart and develop secure attachments.

A qualified coach who practices Positive Psychology can be that consistent and reliable attachment for you. They will ask powerful questions that steer you away from self-judgment and shame, and toward meaningful recovery. Beginning to consider your future is a step toward expanding your options beyond the present. Your future hopes *can* live side-by-side with the past and present as long as they are all in balance. By identifying your values and priorities, you can focus on what you really want and desire as part of a sustainable recovery. Here are a few examples of heart-opening questions:

- What brings you contentment?
- What do you really want and desire?
- If you could have three wishes granted, what would they be?

Not easy questions, but they open the door to a soul-searching process. As my coach, Sandra "Sam" Foster, shared with me: "It's not that anything *has* to happen, but simply what *could* happen." This idea has always resonated with me, because it takes the pressure off and lets me work toward the mere potential of success. As a list-making, goal-oriented perfectionist in recovery, I need to be reminded to relax and just envision an ideal life rather than have it all mapped out. Moving from the narrow world of addiction to the expansive horizon of recovery opens you up to many possibilities.

Values Clarification

Sam believed in me when I had trouble believing in myself. Having a trusted coach or confidant in your corner helps you realize there are people out there you can count on. Once you start to envision a brighter future, it's time to clarify your core values through a simple exercise such as the following:

Coach: *Without overthinking it, answer the following question with the first thing that pops into your mind. What matters most to you?*

Client: *My children and my spouse.*

Coach: *What else?*

Client: *Staying clean and sober and living with integrity.*

Coach: *What else?*

Client: *Being of service to family and friends.*

Coach: *What else?*

The exercise continues until you run out of answers. It's almost like wringing out a wet towel. The point of clarifying your values is to identify the vital parts of who you are. Your belief system got muted during active addiction, and often remains quiet in early recovery. But when you unearth your authentic values, they provide direction for goals and actions, and in turn help you feel more competent.

Our values define who we are. Each person comes into recovery with a different healing template, but only two possibilities emerge. If your values are congruent with your recovery goals and actions, you'll feel energized, optimistic, and hopeful. The possibilities will be endless. But if your values are not congruent with your goals and actions, you'll feel stuck, hopeless, and depressed. Congruency fosters sustainable recovery, which shows up only when you're in sync with your deepest values.

In this next chapter of your recovery, what matters most to you?

Alex: *Developing a loving relationship with myself.*

Mario: *Continuing this path of feeling comfortable and at ease, and feeling good about who I am.*

Colin: *To deepen my relationship with God. I think the first five years of recovery was just getting back on my feet, getting grounded, and getting away from harmful addiction patterns. The cutting edge for me is forming a partnership and deepening a romantic relationship.*

Susan: *I have a list of goals. I'm writing a book and going back to grad school. I want to find my life partner and be as healthy as I can.*

Seth: *Obtaining a higher level of serenity and some inner peace. I still struggle with discontent—the work I want to do is toward that. More acceptance of where I am in my life, and to not get so caught up in the little things.*

The terms religion and spirituality are often used interchangeably, but for our purposes, let's focus on spirituality as applied to sexual addiction. Many years ago, I attended a presentation given by a UCLA chaplain titled "Addiction and Spirituality." He offered the definition of spirituality I've been using ever since, stating that spirituality is "whatever gives your life meaning." Because there's so much fear and misconception about spirituality, I share this simple yet powerful definition whenever I can. It leaves plenty of room to consider what's meaningful to you without religious pressure or innuendo. You might say it offers a blank spiritual canvas.

In my previous book, *From Now On*, I focused on your sense of purpose. I believe purpose provides a necessary foundation for long-term recovery. In my case, loving relationships have always been a lifesaver, so I chose to pursue a career in social work and psychotherapy, letting my conviction to help others learn about themselves and develop more satisfying relationships become my purpose. Though relationships are hard work, they constantly teach me about myself, and allow me to assist others in learning about themselves. By asking yourself questions related to your purpose, you can envision what may lie ahead and develop a sense of mission. At first, there may be more questions than answers. That's okay. For now, I'm just asking you to be curious, nonjudgmental, and to let go of the outcome.

When I was doing hospice work in the early 1990s, I worked with another chaplain (yes, several chaplains have offered me their wisdom). He told me that purpose doesn't reveal itself unless we ask the bigger questions of life, and I believe recovery can only gain traction when these questions are pondered.

Several years ago, I watched a documentary about rabbis in Jerusalem who love to debate, confront, and investigate complicated spiritual questions. What intrigued me was that they never arrive at crystal clear answers. So is it necessary for you to arrive at concrete answers in your recovery? I've come to realize that recovery is not so neat and tidy. It requires you to be humble about your own hopes and failings, and remain curious about healthy ways to engage with the world. Let's look at an example.

Case Study Seven: Miguel's Reason to Wake up in the Morning

Miguel always pressured himself to be liked by everyone. His mother died when he was ten years old, and they had been very close. He was raised by a single dad who struggled to connect with his only child; they grieved side by side, but never seemed to bond directly. Miguel was hungry for a father who would spend time with him, but the only thing they had in common was the loss of a loved one.

In school Miguel became a favorite of his teachers and coaches. They were all aware of his loss, and he enjoyed the extra attention he received. He worked hard, and in spite of his mother's death, he earned good grades and made the varsity baseball team in high school. But when he left for college, something changed. He was no longer a big fish in a small pond. He felt lost in the crowd at the state university. At first, Miguel withdrew and felt homesick, but then as he hung out more with teammates, his sense of belonging slowly formed. On the advice of a teammate, he learned how to binge eat and purge to keep his weight down for the baseball season. He felt more confident when he kept the weight off.

As college unfolded, he became a regular at the local bars and grew skillful at picking up girls. He was hooking up multiple times a week. This new *hobby* gave him a sense of confidence, but his bulimia worsened.

"I only felt good if my body was just right," he recalls. "If I had washboard abs I felt better about myself and would pick up more girls. It was a vicious cycle."

After college Miguel started working as an assistant coach in the minor leagues with the intention to move up the ranks someday. Unfortunately, his sexual acting out spun out of control. He would call in sick after being out late the night before. Miguel became distracted and depleted, and eventually he was fired.

"Every day I woke up anxious and obsessing about my next opportunity to act out," Miguel says. "My drugs of choice were anonymous sex and binge eating, but whatever would get me out of my pain was on the table. Eventually it got so bad that I would do *anything* to feel better. Fortunately, that's when I found the program. The twelve-steps saved my life."

With the help of a friend, Miguel went to his first meeting of Sex Addicts Anonymous. He knew immediately that he was in the right place. He'd found like-minded people, and became a regular at several meetings. Miguel felt grateful for the new sober community and took commitments at his meetings. He worked the steps with a sponsor, and eventually sponsored others.

After two years in the program, Miguel believed it was time to focus on a career. In spite of his distractions, Miguel's grades were always solid, and he was told that he had a good chance of getting into a strong graduate school program. Miguel decided to earn a master's in business administration, focusing his studies on nonprofit management. His school provided career coaching that helped him clarify his values and goals, and with the help of this career coach, he discovered a direction congruent with his heart's desire.

After business school, Miguel put together a coalition of mental health providers to create an organization for children who have suffered the death of a loved one. He hadn't gotten the grief support he longed for as a child, so he felt determined to develop a program that fulfilled this need in his community.

"I don't know exactly where this is going to take me," says Miguel, "but for the first time I feel a passion and purpose like I've never felt before. It just feels right in my heart, and it truly gives me a reason to wake up in the morning. My recovery has opened up a clear direction for my life, and I don't want to blow this chance."

Miguel converted his loss into his calling. Sex and food no longer run the show—his newfound focus is on giving back to others and creating a life worth living.

Life Contentment

The following exercise is a chance for you to list your priorities in life at this moment in time. Rate the following areas of your life as you experience them today on a scale from 0 to 5 (0 being the least content, and 5 being the most content):

Career/School:	Home:	Emotional Health:
Money:	Love and Romance:	Sexual Health:
Friends:	Fun and Play:	Spiritual Health:
Family:	Physical Health:	

Once you've ranked each of these areas, ask yourself the following questions and share your answers with a trusted confidant:

- Which of these areas are my highest priorities? Choose three.
- What is my top priority?

- What matters most to me and my recovery at this time? How can I establish goals and action steps congruent with these priorities?

What are your highest priorities at this time?

Seth: *To stay sober. Also, my kids and my partner.*

Colin: *My connection with my Higher Power. Building my new career. Growing friendships and maintaining strong family relationships.*

Alex: *I want to be healthy. I'm really into drinking water and brushing my teeth, flossing, exercising every day, calling my sponsor every day. Those things have to be done in order to keep me safe and sane.*

Robert: *Sanity.*

Dr. Seligman coined the acronym PERMA to list the elements of life satisfaction:

Positive Emotion: Seeing your life in a positive light.

Engagement: Immersion in your favorite activities.

Relationships: Meaningful social and intimate connections.

Meaning: Being of service to others and your community.

Accomplishments: Setting goals that offer you a sense of achievement.

From a recovery perspective, you can see how these elements are necessary for building a capacity for vitality, buoyancy, and resiliency. Somewhat surprisingly, Dr. Seligman found positive emotion to be the least important element of the PERMA model. Instead, being engaged in your life and being of service were the most essential components to life satisfaction. This surprised me, but Positive Psychology is not all about happiness. It is concerned more with engagement and meaning, deeper contact and purpose.

Take the example of Walt Disney. A pioneer in the entertainment industry, he of course created "the Happiest Place on Earth" and built an empire around his vision. That level of engagement, purpose, and meaning is tremendous. Now you may not have the resources to create an empire, but you do have the wherewithal and inner capacity to develop your own version of deeper connection and purpose in life. Disney assembled a team of like-minded people and followed his extraordinary vision, which resulted in the world of Disney we know today.

The celebrated author and motivational speaker Jack Canfield is another proponent of "visioning"—a deliberate exercise to take stock of where you are, while imagining a more expansive life. You might restrain yourself to a smaller vision just because change is scary. But long-term recovery is about growth—being as big as you truly are. Pace yourself. Follow your rhythm within, but try not to limit yourself. Remember Sam Foster's reminder: "It's not that anything has to happen, but simply what *could* happen."

Visioning

Do you know what you really want? You've already evaluated your satisfaction level in the following areas of your life. Now without overthinking it, jot down your vision for each one. Take your time and do this in a quiet space. Bring your journal with you on a hike, to a coffeehouse, or onto your back patio perhaps. Don't hold back just because you think the goals are not possible right now.

The idea behind this visioning exercise is to give shape and voice to your vision of life and recovery *one year from now*. Be sure to give yourself plenty of time to ponder each of these issues before writing. I also recommend you do the exercise longhand rather than on a computer. Using a pen and paper will slow you down and let you savor the experience more fully.

Career/School:	Physical Health:	Fun and Play:
Finances:	Emotional Health:	Home:
Friends:	Sexual Health:	Love and Romance:
Family:	Spiritual Health:	

The visioning exercise benefits from you allowing time and space for self-exploration. Take at least a week or two to consider these possibilities before sharing them with a trustworthy person. Sharing your vision is an intimate experience. Refer back to the exercise from time to time to build perspective on where you are and where you see yourself going.

Visioning lays the groundwork for the next chapter of your recovery. But without clear action steps, these new goals remain conceptual. Say, for example, you've identified family as a core value, yet know you've been out of touch with your youngest son for the past few years. How exactly will you reengage with his life? Perhaps you'll volunteer as umpire for his little league baseball team. What concrete action step will create that involvement? Talk to your son and the coach to find out.

Here is another example of a specific goal and action steps to support greater accountability:

Physical Health Goal: To lose ten pounds in five months.

Action Steps:

- Research a nutritional plan that is healthy and attainable.
- Attend weekly Overeaters Anonymous meeting.
- Work out three times a week with a friend.
- Do cardiovascular exercise twenty minutes daily.
- Attend a monthly nutritionist appointment.
- Eliminate refined sugar and unnecessary carbohydrates from your diet.

Proving to yourself that you can master new daily routines can be a major breakthrough in itself. It's been said that it takes twenty-one days to introduce a new habit into the rhythm of your life. So what small actions can you complete every day to support your recovery? Self-care is one way to build the infrastructure for more ambitious action steps. Listen to a relaxation app nightly. Play your favorite music. Write a gratitude list daily.

As I stated in Chapter Four, active addiction occurs in a narrow, narcissistic box, so recovery suggests that you be of service to others. Below is one way to align your priorities with purposeful goals and action steps. This is an example of how you might identify a top priority, such as getting more involved in your community:

Highest Priorities (as listed in the Life Contentment Exercise):

- Family
- Community
- Contribution

Purposeful Goal (community-related): Organize local committee to explore options to clean up city parks.

Action Steps:

- Block out two to four hours a week for volunteering.
- Invite family and neighbors to participate in this project.
- Collaborate with City Parks and Recreation coordinator to advertise through social media.
- Check in with an accountability person weekly regarding progress.
- Designate a park cleanup day by the end of the year.

Now return to your Life Contentment Exercise and pull your highest priorities. Feel free to focus on just one or to consider all three. Pace yourself. And keep in mind that a high priority is a goal that you would like to focus on *right away*. Here are some reminders about setting up goals.

Goals become purposeful when you:

1. Align your core values with your goals and action steps.
2. Stretch beyond your comfort zone and set yourself up for success.
3. Surround yourself with like-minded, positive people.
4. Declare your intentions publicly to confidants.
5. Visualize the end result.
6. Reward yourself upon completion.

Once your action steps and goals align with your values and intentions, your energy flows. In the example I presented, the park cleanup project met the individual's values of family, community, and contribution, thus supporting his core beliefs and creating more ease and motivation in his daily life. As you commit to your values and seek accountability from others, don't be afraid to ask for help, or even just a reassuring hug, to feel less alone.

Yet how do you ask for help if it doesn't come naturally to you? Think of a time when a friend asked for your assistance with something that is easy for you. How did it feel as you helped them? How did that affect your friendship? And how did you feel about yourself afterward? Most likely this was a positive, bonding experience for you. Now that you've imagined being on the giving end, what stops you from being on the receiving end? What gets in the way of you asking for help? Seize the opportunity to depend on dependable people. The results may surprise you and turn out to be mutually satisfying. Giving and receiving help is a fundamental part of sexual recovery, one that builds more secure attachments.

Everyone has challenges giving and receiving love; it's emotionally risky. Some people are more comfortable with giving, others prefer receiving. As you work toward your goals, you will need emotionally reliable people for support. So who would you like to ask? A close friend? Sponsor? Therapist? Coach? You may find yourself with more than one accountability person. An accountability team is helpful, as long as you're all on the same page. Kids often choose one parent to ask for something, and when they don't get it, they try the other parent. Don't let the little kid in you go searching for a more pliant ally. Personal accountability is what counts, and it has more dimensionality when it involves multiple people and, if applicable, a Higher Power.

Another accountability tool is writing. Keep a journal of your feelings, thoughts, ideas, and memories to promote a sense of structure and tracking. Identify your strengths and leverage them. Recognize your limitations and seek help in overcoming them. If you are prone to procrastination, find someone who can help you stay on track. Most of all—I can't emphasize this enough—*don't go it alone.*

Swimming with the Dolphins

In her book *The Wealthy Spirit*, author Chellie Campbell adopts a brilliant sea metaphor as she suggests that you surround yourself with dolphins.

Her financial stress reduction workshop teaches students that there are *your people*, and the rest of the world; it's your job in life to find your pod. If you have too much of a need to be liked by others, this will cause suffering. Campbell explains that there are three types of people in the world:

1. *Dolphins swim together in harmony. They are clever, playful, and communicate exceptionally well. They cooperate during hunts and are protective of one another.*
2. *Sharks bite you when you least expect it. They tend to attack when they feel threatened, and require a safe space around them.*
3. *Tuna get eaten by others. They don't have much backbone and blame others for their misfortune. Tuna also tend to be needy.*

Take a moment to identify the sharks and tuna in your life. Who are they?

Who are your dolphins, those people who love you no matter what? You need to continue nurturing these relationships for the times when you feel vulnerable. Life is too short to waste swimming with sharks and tuna, but of course we all possess fishy qualities. Once you identify the unproductive characteristics in yourself, you're more likely to identify them in others. In a way, acknowledging who the dolphins are in your life is like expressing gratitude. Counting your blessings on a regular basis is another tool that Positive Psychologists say contributes to contentment.

What are you most grateful for in your life today?

Seth: *I'm most grateful for my recovery because everything that is good in my life has followed from that process.*

Colin: *To have a second shot at life. To have a different experience of life today. But most importantly, and what makes all of that possible, is having a conscious connection with a power greater than myself.*

Mario: *That I'm present. That I can see how wonderful my life is, instead of chasing after all of the things that could have happened.*

Robert: *I'm grateful for my relationships, including the*
relationship with myself, my Higher Power, my friends,
my family. Grateful for my job, my home, and my health.
Alex: *The fact that I didn't get HIV, because I know I could have.*

Gratitude has received newfound attention because it's such a simple and impactful practice. Everyone, from Oprah to the twelve-step community to Positive Psychologists, is teaching its benefits. Sonja Lyubomirsky, PhD, a psychologist and author, shares the following ways gratitude boosts happiness in her book *The How of Happiness*: gratitude magnifies fulfilling life events, helps you feel better about yourself, and is useful to balance out the negative effects of disappointing experiences. By reminding yourself of what you're grateful for in your recovery, you'll build perspective against what hasn't gone right in your life. Tracking gratitude also builds your capacity for deeper connections with others and decreases your tendency toward shame and comparison.

Dr. Seligman suggests specific action steps to promote an "attitude of gratitude": Begin by writing down three things you're grateful for every day before going to sleep. Secondly, write a gratitude letter to someone who has positively impacted you, and deliver the letter directly to the person to savor the experience. Write about three different times in your life when one door closed, and another door opened as a result of that ending or loss. Design a perfect day for yourself—an ideal field trip that feeds your soul. Write about it throughout the day and share what you wrote with someone you trust. Set aside a specific day to do something generous. Ask a friend or family member to write a letter describing how they see you impacting their future.

Gratitude leads to inner vitality. It energizes you and teaches your neural pathways that a positive charge is sustainable. Implement those of Dr. Seligman's suggestions that resonate most for you.

How do you experience vitality in your recovery today?

Mario: *I want to learn more, and learn about different things, in*
a genuinely interested way—not in a compulsive way.

Colin: *Vitality was not a feeling I had for the first thirty-five years of my life pre-recovery. Now I'm more productive at work and also pursuing a new career path, am present and available for the people in my life, have the energy and desire to do things I enjoy, and continue to grow and expand.*

Seth: *In recovery I have a lot of passion. I dance, I hike—I still have a pretty youthful spirit.*

Susan: *The other day I found myself running like a little kid, just for fun. I don't see a lot of forty-eight-year-olds doing that. I run for joy.*

Contentment, gratitude, love. All of these are elements of purposeful recovery. As you build a capacity for a bigger life, savor the pleasant moments and see how they nourish your overall sense of well-being and hope.

Action Steps:

1. Positive Psychologists introduced new strategies perfectly adaptable for addiction recovery. Identify your character assets and share them with a confidant.

2. Core values emerge when you ask yourself, "What matters most to me?" Meaning and purpose also take shape once you clarify your values.

3. Identify your three highest priorities by using the Life Contentment Exercise. They provide a compass toward purposeful goals and actions.

4. Take time to write down your vision. Don't rush—give yourself space and time to soak in the exercise.

5. Name the dolphins in your life and increase contact with them. By spending time with your pod, anxiety will diminish, and a sense of connection will flourish in its place.

6. Count your blessings every day. Keep a gratitude journal and share these revelations with loved ones. Focus on what's going right and ask for help when things go wrong.

Chapter Eight

Sexual Healing

Sex is emotion in motion.
—Mae West

In addition to pleasure and procreation, sex is about connection. But at some point, compulsive sex hijacked your brain as you searched solely for the physical high. Even when you wanted to stop, you couldn't, and the consequences became more complicated and severe. You may have contracted a disease, lost relationships, or spent inordinate amounts of time and money supporting your addiction. Even now, when it comes to sex, do you lean toward relationships, or hide from human connection? Pursue intimacy, or run for the hills? Sex addiction presents a dilemma— the isolation is lonely, but emotional intimacy scares you. Recognizing your sexual and sensual choices may inspire you to express yourself fully.

In early recovery, you focused on minimizing your compulsive behaviors; now that they've been tamed, it's time to safely and productively enjoy sober sex—without the influence of mind-altering behaviors from the past.

The World Health Organization defines sexual health as "a state of physical, mental, and social well-being in relation to sexuality. It requires a positive and respectful approach to sexuality and sexual relationships, as well as the possibility of having pleasurable and safe sexual experiences, free of coercion, discrimination, and violence." In sexual recovery you get to determine what a positive, respectful, pleasurable, and safe experience is for you. This can be a very personal and sacred time of self-exploration, and I encourage you to stay openhearted.

Your Erotic Template

Before you explore your erotic desires, however, it's best to recognize your sexual blueprint. Share your desires, turn-ons, longings, and fantasies with a trusted confidant. If you haven't written down your sexual history before, this is the time to do so. After you complete your sex inventory, begin mapping out safer, more fulfilling sexual possibilities to consider adding in this next chapter of your recovery, whether you're single or partnered.

By fully examining your erotic template, you'll find ways to infuse playful, imaginative, and spontaneous qualities into your menu of sexual options. Sexual healing also requires serious reflection on your triggers toward compulsive sex, in order to understand how the addiction became so entrenched in the first place. Your out-of-control sexual behaviors thrived because of the supercharged rush and immediate gratification that came along with them. You know that much. But it's also important to understand the thoughts and feelings that caused these lustful urges.

Every one of your emotions can trigger you to act out sexually—anger, hurt, sadness, fear, disappointment, shame, and even joy. To begin, take a close look at your anger. How would you describe it? Anger sometimes gets a bad rap. For all its dangers, it is a life force and source of energy that lets others know what's unacceptable to you. If unexpressed, anger can fuel compulsive sex. It's an attempt to protect your inner child, which never was fully protected, and there's intelligence, wisdom, and love in anger that is also integral to your sexuality. If you fully accept your anger and a sexual partner embraces it, this emotion can enhance sexual heat. Do your best to express your anger directly, honestly, and clearly—not in punishing or self-punishing ways that sabotage intimacy.

Sexual acting out was a deliberate effort to be messy and break rules. For rule-abiding perfectionists, having a teenage rebellion was a necessary phase that you may have missed and then expressed through compulsive sex. It served a purpose, but has since outlasted its welcome. In order to heal from your childhood wounds, all of you—your anger, sexuality, pain, love—needs to be expressed fully.

If your inner critic has been a powerful force through the years, it's time to let go of the self-judgment once and for all. The harder you are on yourself, the more sexually compulsive you feel. In other words, the more you believe sex to be bad, the more likely you are to act out. Because self-loathing and self-judgment are protective and distancing, they block opportunities for intimate sex. Work instead toward shame resiliency and self-acceptance; you'll create more possibilities for sexual health and, eventually, deeply connected sex.

But getting closer to others may also come with feelings of superiority and judgmental thoughts toward others. Ask yourself why you're reacting this way. Whatever quality in the other person caused this reaction actually reflects something about you; see the trigger as a mirror. Notice when this part—sometimes referred to as your shadow—is activated. This shadow side of you is often unseen and disowned. Acknowledge it as vital information. Usually, it will show up in self-protective behavior, such as blame. Your job now is to explore what you're really protecting yourself from.

When you identify and own your shadow parts, your recovery becomes more dimensional, which is to say more serious and complex. For example, if you now recognize when you're being judgmental, you have ventured from self-centeredness toward humility. In order to proceed from less judgment toward love, try listing everything about a relationship in your life that irritates you. It's crucial that you feel all of the feelings without doing a spiritual bypass. Seriously. Give yourself plenty of time to brainstorm everything that bothers you about them. Owning your aggression allows you to fully express yourself rather than mute your feelings. By expressing unexpressed anger, you practice relapse prevention and create an open channel for intimacy and sexual connection.

After you've given yourself the time and space to let out your resentments and rage, you can track your generosity of spirit, through which you'll feel freer to share yourself with others emotionally and sexually. By purging those emotions associated with judgment and superiority, you prepare to harness your better nature. Hopefully you'll have a new experience of lightness and perspective that allows you to see others, and yourself, as human, which is to say acceptably flawed.

In American culture, we often confuse sex with love, and we'll explore this misunderstanding more later on, but for now let's take a look at how they intersect. Sexual arousal is beautiful; what you do with it is another thing. Tracking sexual energy can be a sophisticated way of getting to know the cues in your body. One way of doing this is through chakras.

In Buddhism and Hinduism, chakras are thought of as wheels in your body where energy flows. Of the seven chakras, two get the most attention when it comes to sex and love addiction. The first is the sacral chakra. Located in the pelvic area, it controls your openness to new experiences and your ability to accept and connect with others. The sacral chakra also holds emotional issues, well-being, pleasure, and sexuality. The second is the heart chakra, the center for your ability to love, and the location of joy and inner peace. It's possible to move your sexual energy from the sacral chakra to the heart chakra at any given time, but it takes diligent practice and intention to shift your energy and thus convert sexual energy into love. Paying attention to both chakras simultaneously creates the possibility for the integration of sex and intimacy.

Sexual healing is a quest to meet unmet emotional needs. Feeling understood, valued, and desired by sexual partners is vital for deeply connected sex to flourish, but sex without love compartmentalizes pleasure and emotion, shutting out the potential for intimate feelings. With that said, your sober sex life is up to you—pleasurable, consensual sex is possible in a one-time hook-up or between life partners. As you clarify what fits best for you, notice your level of satisfaction with sexual experiences in whatever shape or form they take.

Although sexual desire can sometimes be fueled by risk and danger, intimacy can actually be one of the greatest risks of all. If you tend to be the distancer in your relationship (most sex addicts are), intimacy may sound appealing and terrifying at the same time. In choosing to pursue your sexual partner and have a more loving relationship, you'll reveal more of yourself, leaving you feeling exposed. But without emotional risk-taking and vulnerability, there is no prospect for greater intimacy.

Hotter sex also requires relaxation and trust. It's impossible to truly relax with someone unless you trust them, and it's impossible to trust someone until you can relax with them. Because true comfort with a person of interest takes time and practice, begin by noticing when you feel more or less relaxed. Listen to your nervous system; it offers clues to your level of emotional safety and blossoming trust. Remember, building trust is a process, and one not to be taken lightly. As you get to know someone, trust will develop over time, not overnight.

Sustainable recovery allows you to reclaim sexual vitality. Although compulsive sex seemed exciting at the time, it deadened your soul. But when you resuscitate your mind, body, and spirit, your life energy will return.

We often discuss sexual vitality in the context of sexual performance, but if we broaden the definition, it can also refer to vibrant sexual health. For instance, many sex addicts, and people in general, tend to be focused primarily on the orgasm, but sexual vitality encompasses a more embodied approach, including touching, kissing, and overall verbal and nonverbal connection. Let's see how one gets to this point by looking at the example of my client Alexander and his sponsor Joseph.

Case Study Eight: Alexander's Path toward Sober Sex

Alexander recently attended his first meeting of Sexual Compulsives Anonymous and heard someone share about "sober sex." The phrase both piqued his interest and intimidated him at the same time. He got that it had something to do with sexual recovery, but couldn't conceptualize what it would eventually mean to him.

Alexander had known he was gay since about the age of eight. But having grown up in rural South Dakota, he didn't feel safe coming out of the closet until he went away to college in Minnesota. Alexander didn't just step out of the closet, then. He ran out. He explored his sexual identity through LGBTQ events on campus, and discovered hook-up apps. On campus, he became politically active. At night he would look for sex online or at the gay bars. When there was a night without a hook-up, he would spend inordinate amounts of time watching porn.

At first, Alexander felt like a sexual explorer going on new adventures every day. He was learning about himself and found the hook-ups stimulating. Over time, he gave up on the bar scene and only met guys online; this was more efficient for him. Checking apps for the pursuit of the night became an obsessive habit. What started out as a fun way to explore his sexual possibilities escalated out of control. He wanted to stop, but couldn't.

Little by little, he took more risks. He scared himself when he started to have unprotected sex with anonymous partners. Alexander made an appointment at the college counseling center and spoke to someone about his out-of-control urges. His counselor told him about the predominantly gay twelve-step program called Sexual Compulsives Anonymous (SCA). Alexander thought its description fit him to a T.

He found a meeting at the city's LGBTQ center. He sat in a circle with a dozen other men who identified themselves as sexually compulsive. It was a speaker meeting. A middle-aged man named Joseph talked, referring to his twenties as his "lost decade."

"Those ten years were a blur," he explained. "I was on the prowl every day, be it online, in bathhouses, or with escorts. At some point it didn't matter how I got off. I just had to get off one way or another every day."

Joseph's honesty and clarity engrossed Alexander. He'd never heard someone share their sexual exploits so openly. Immediately, he felt less alone and less shameful about his compulsive behavior. Joseph continued: "It's been three years since I've had sex outside of my marriage, and I feel like a different person. My husband now sees me as a reliable and consistent partner instead of someone full of secrets and lies."

Joseph's story was a cautionary tale for Alexander, who was still in his early twenties. After the meeting, Alexander asked Joseph to be his temporary sponsor. He was impressed by Joseph's commitment to his recovery and his marriage, and felt like he'd found a role model unlike anyone he'd known back in South Dakota.

Joseph told Alexander, "I had to learn how to bring sex and intimacy together in my relationship. This was no easy process. I was used to going outside my relationship for sex. The idea of 'sober sex' was foreign to me. So we went to a sex therapist and began talking about what sex really means to us. We came up with an agreed-upon vision for our sex life, which became our mutual understanding of deeply connected sex. We have a long way to go still, but we're both committed to it, and to one another."

Alexander admired Joseph's bravery, his vulnerability and willingness to work toward emotional intimacy, even going so far as to seek outside help with his partner.

"Seeing Joseph do this in his relationship gives me courage to talk about it with my counselor," Alexander says. "I don't have to wait till I'm in a relationship to look at my healthy sexual desires and consider safer ways to express them."

Do you believe you're a healthy sexual being? If so, how? If not, why not?

Alex: *I would like to be with somebody who I have a strong sexual connection with and know well. That hasn't happened, so it's not ideal right now, but I think for me to not have sex, which I've done before, is not healthy.*

Robert: *The most important thing is that I've let go of a lot of shame. Of course I still make mistakes. I still have a lot of insecurities and uncertainties, but I don't let them rule my sexuality anymore. I am much more present in my sexual life today.*

Mario: *By engaging only in sexual activities with my partner because I made a monogamous choice—we don't keep secrets—and accepting who I am, imperfections and all, I have a healthy, emotional connection.*

Colin: *For me, what that looks like is being more conscious about my sexual activity—Is it enhancing my life? Is it depleting my life?*

Susan: *One of the gifts of SLAA (Sex and Love Addicts*
              Anonymous) is I had this relationship that didn't work out,
              but he introduced me to tantra and it was magnificent.
              Meditating first, getting grounded and centered, sitting and
              practicing breathing before getting sexual, is a wonderful
              practice. In the past I would disassociate and try to recreate
              the trauma in my sex life. Now I don't want that. I just
              want gentleness, kindness, presence of mind and body.

Seth: *I still struggle with vulnerability, with initiating sex, and*
              to feel comfortable being sexual. A lot of that revolves
              around my own internalized homophobia—there's still a
              part of me that keeps saying at some level it's wrong, or I
              shouldn't be doing this or whatever. That gets in my way.

Abstinence is not a sustainable approach to sexual sobriety, especially in the long term. The combination of sex and intimacy can be the most sustainable path. But there are also ways to enjoy sexual pleasure without intimacy. Your sexual repertoire is yours to safely explore. For example, you may choose to work with a qualified surrogate partner, a practitioner who focuses on issues of intimacy and sexuality. With the surrogate, you participate in experiential exercises that are sensual and sometimes sexual. You then process these experiences with a collaborative psychotherapist. If this option feels too overwhelming for you, it's not the time to consider it. Proceed with caution, discuss your situation with a licensed psychotherapist or clinical sexologist, and keep in mind that sexual health embraces positive, respectful, safe, and pleasurable sexual experiences. If you choose to pursue an outside-the-box option, be sure to get your referrals from someone you trust.

The integration of sex, love, and intimacy is a lifelong process. Don't feel stressed if it doesn't happen right away, and if you're feeling stuck and would like to explore your sexual health further, find a qualified sex coach, an AASECT-certified sex therapist, or a licensed psychotherapist who specializes in sexual healing. Always do your research and meet with them for a consultation, if possible. See the Resources section in the back of the book for helpful websites.

How do you integrate sex and intimacy?

Susan: *Take it slow. I had relationships where I jumped right into the sex, but I've learned that if I go slow and connect with someone on an emotional and spiritual level first, the physical stuff will be much better.*

Mario: *By only engaging in sexual activity with somebody who knows and accepts me for who I am. I show up as a person and they show up as a person, not as a fantasy, or a stand-in for porn.*

Alex: *I'm not there yet. When I have sex, it's with somebody that I like. I don't necessarily know them completely. I want to reach the point when I'm able to say that I love the person I'm having sex with.*

Healthy Fantasy

Fantasy often gets shortchanged in twelve-step rooms, where it's typically linked to problematic behaviors such as compulsive porn use or love addiction. Some of you may even call yourself a fantasy addict. But sexual recovery opens the door for healthy fantasies that can enrich your sexual vitality. This is precarious terrain, so go slow, and get lots of reality checks from your sponsor or therapist. For example, you may find yourself fantasizing about a coworker. Instead of trying to eliminate these sexual thoughts, share them with your therapist so you don't have to keep the fantasy a secret or shame yourself for it.

Exploring your sexual imagination allows for new sexual possibilities, even if they're never acted on. Starting to fantasize about expanding your sexual repertoire can be life affirming, self-loving, and frightening. In your past, this energy was put toward something compulsive, like porn. Now it's time to use your sexual imagination to learn about yourself. Fantasy serves the vital purpose of providing sexual arousal, sparking curiosity, revealing taboos, providing relaxation, and even builds sexual confidence.

By freely sharing your sexual history with someone you trust, you replace the isolation and secrecy of the past with transparency. It's a vulnerable thing to give yourself the sexual freedom to experience trial and error. Stay open and accountable, and you'll feel more emotionally sober as you design an upgraded sexual vision and heal the shame others have given you.

All sex addicts get lost in fantasy. How is fantasy a part of your life today?

Colin: *That is tricky for me. In my addictive pre-recovery days, fantasy was a way of escaping. Today fantasy can be a way to consider new possibilities for my sex life. But it's something I need to be mindful about, because it's in the same part of my brain that went into unhealthy fantasy territory. I need to be mindful that I'm not using it to avoid dealing with something deeper in my life.*

Susan: *In meetings I identify myself as a sex, love, and fantasy addict because I spent most of my life in either grandiosity—over-the-top positive fantasy—or really negative, dark fantasy. A sponsor told me to invite God into my masturbation practice. I'd say, God, there's nobody in my life right now, can we just have sex? Inviting that Higher Power into my body is a healthy fantasy, as opposed to thinking about that person who hurts you every time you get together.*

Your erotic template is the part of your life force based on your unique wants and desires. For sex addicts, however, the road back to an erotic template can be a glacial one. Consider very carefully what are safe, fun, and liberating sexual expressions. In twelve-step rooms there can be a lot of focus on what *not* to do. Erotic desires and fantasies are often taboo subjects, in part because they may trigger others. Utilize a trusted confidant, a highly qualified therapist or open-minded sponsor, to share honest, vulnerable sexual conversations. Ask yourself directly: What are my greatest sexual desires? What is most satisfying about my sex life today? What feels shameful about my sexual expression? What is it about sex that feels most free and liberating? Does intimacy need to be part of sex for me? How do I envision my future sex life?

If remnants of puritanical messaging still reside in you, provocative questions like these may be but rarely explored. Your erotic self can get overshadowed by so-called "higher priorities," but sex is an essential part of your well-being and vitality. Exploring your erotic template in a responsible way will raise your consciousness toward more mindful sexual choices, reducing your vulnerability to relapse. Update your sexual boundaries as you decide what's sexually enriching, as opposed to what's compulsive.

Mindful Sex

It's impossible to have a satisfying sex life without being in the moment. So how do you find your way there? Establish a mindfulness practice that allows you to be as fully present during sex as possible. It's only human to drift away from the sexual moment at times, but finding your way back more efficiently will feel more satisfying.

Notice when you seem to drift away from your sexual partner. Try to be curious and nonjudgmental as you find your way back. For those of you who are used to disconnecting (sometimes called dissociating), be especially patient as you build more sexual awareness. There is no cookie-cutter approach to mindful sex, so it may take some experimentation to find what works best for you.

Ironically, compulsive sex often leads to frozenness in your body. The nervous system becomes dysregulated from high levels of arousal. As a result, your body is disengaged from the sexual experience in the here and now. Your mind is so focused on achieving orgasm, the rest of your body gets ignored. If you want to integrate physical and emotional intimacy, the therapeutic direction is to regulate your nervous system through greater somatic awareness and safe, trusting personal connection to others. It will take time, but your system will thaw as you develop more capacity to live in the moment.

Sexual compulsivity required compartmentalizing—living a double life, keeping secrets, and constructing impenetrable walls between sex and love. Yet humans are social creatures, wired for connection, and when you integrate sex and intimacy, your brain and body will thank you for it.

Revisiting Safer Sex

In the 1980s, the concept of "safer sex" was developed in response to the AIDS crisis. It may be true that the only "safe sex" is abstinence; all forms of sex carry some degree of risk. But abstaining from sex is neither realistic nor desirable. Back in that time of uncertainty and fear, society endorsed cautious sexual choices. Today, nearly forty years later, the dilemma still lingers. How do you define "safer sex" in the context of your recovery?

Without letting go of the importance of STD prevention methods, consider opening up your definition of safer sex. You may also consider looking into sensual experiences such as cuddle parties, massage exchange, improvisational dance, or partner yoga—all options to move toward body awareness, relaxation, and safer touch. It's nearly impossible to have truly fulfilling sex without relaxing your body.

Masturbating in moderation can also provide relaxation as you explore self-touch as a fun, pleasurable choice. Yet it's another controversial topic for sex addicts. When not done compulsively, masturbation is a means of sexual self-care. Masturbation can be a loving, safe, self-appreciative way to enjoy yourself when you are truly mindful. In the past, masturbation often became habitual and hyperfocused on porn images rather than focused on the pleasure in your body. Because the mind absorbs images like a sponge, too much exposure to porn can make it the primary erotic turn-on, getting in the way of the pleasure of real-life sex. Enter this territory gradually if you masturbated compulsively in the past. Discuss your self-pleasuring habits with a sponsor or therapist to remove masturbation from the secretive, taboo part of your sexual repertoire. Ease into this sometimes raw discussion, and pace yourself to avoid a shame spiral. Remember, healthier forms of masturbation can be an essential part of sexual vitality and healing.

When do you experience nurturing, safer touch—both sexually and platonically? How is it for you?

Seth: *With my partner, touch feels safe. Sometimes I'll go for a massage, which feels therapeutic. Also, when hugging friends.*

Colin: *I experience healthy, safe touch with a massage therapist I work with who is nurturing, kind (in a non-triggering way), and who takes care of me in ways that I haven't experienced before. I also experience it with brothers in the program when we exchange hugs after meetings. I experience it with the hugs and kisses I get from my niece and nephew, my family members, and in healthy relationships with women where touch is not sexualized but in a way that's affirming, nurturing, and loving.*

Mario: *It feels great that touch is possible as a nurturing activity instead of an adrenaline-filled, rush-producing activity.*

Alex: *I dog-sit a lot, and sometimes I study with the dogs next to me for hours. I sleep with the dogs next to me. I do a lot of that kind of touch because I love animals. That helps me.*

When you were growing up, did you have the "birds and the bees" talk with your parents? Most parents leave sex education to the schools, and that curriculum still seems to boil down to anatomical parts and a rather dry description of traditional heterosexual mating. Depending on when and where you grew up, sex education was likely either lackluster or nonexistent, and you were left on your own to figure things out.

It's not too late to find role models or mentors to have these conversations with. By speaking with a trusted confidant who has more experience and wisdom, you'll give yourself the gift of humility and camaraderie. Sex addiction causes profound isolation. Conversely, sexual recovery helps you develop connections and trust. Ask for the birds and the bees talk from someone you respect; doing so can only repair past sexual wounds.

Who helped you the most to develop healthier forms of sex and intimacy?

Colin: *My sponsor and my brothers in the program who I bounce ideas off. I ask them what's working for them. I check in with them to see if the behavior I'm engaging in is moving me toward more healthy sexual expression and intimacy, or if it's moving me further away from that.*

Seth: *My therapist. We've been working through some of my inner struggles, then we try to bring it back to my relationship.*

Alex: *Right now, nobody. Right now it's just me and my Higher Power.*

Shining the light on your sexual health helps you shift from problematic sexual behaviors to fun, safe, liberating, and playful sexual activities.

Action Steps:
1. Expand your sexual conversations by sharing openly and honestly with a confidant.
2. Discover safe ways to celebrate your sexual self. Keep a log of what feels fun and exploratory, and what feels limiting and depleting.
3. Track moments when you integrate sex and intimacy, as well as times when sex and love are compartmentalized.
4. Take a closer look at your sexual blueprint—those experiences in the past that were most satisfying for you. Don't censor yourself. Notice which memories felt compulsive, and which were relaxing.
5. Be honest with yourself about what works for you sexually or not. List the erotic desires that you want to explore from now on.

Chapter Nine

Breaking down the Walls

There's nothing more intimate in life
than simply being understood.
And understanding someone else.
—Brad Meltzer

Scratch the surface of a sex addict and you'll find a love avoidant. When lost in compulsive sex, you also run away from intimacy. This is not always intentional; a hookup is just so much easier for a love avoidant than dealing with things like trust and respect. We all need intimacy role models. Growing up, your family provides a template for intimate attachment, but most of you didn't receive the love you craved. If they were unavailable, you were left to your own devices. One of the keys to long-term recovery is the integration of sex, love, and intimacy, so in this chapter we'll explore how to achieve this meaningful experience.

The movie *Moulin Rouge* is about challenges with intimacy. Its protagonist desperately seeks someone who is unavailable and potentially life threatening, as he both longs for and fears closeness. His anguish escalates as ongoing attempts to establish a romantic connection with his object of desire prove futile. The obsessive quest for the unobtainable person—sometimes referred to as the *impossible love*—creates emotional hunger and unsatisfied yearning. Giving and receiving love freely is part of the remedy for compulsive sex, and for people longing for intimacy in general. When you develop true intimate contact with others, the addiction wanes and sobriety strengthens.

Dr. Jan Bauer's book *Impossible Love* analyzes both the suffering and the growth that goes on in affairs and other painful romantic entanglements. Although the excitement can be intense, it's unlikely to convert into long-term intimacy. On the plus side, impossible love can be a teaching moment, as you learn about your unmet needs. But only if you recognize these longings, build perspective, and tease out the deeper meaning beneath your obsessions and fantasies can growth occur.

Let's take a closer look at where sustainable love and connection show up in your life. Once again, owning a pet is one of the purest experiences of intimacy; dogs are experts at giving and receiving love. Because of the instinctual way they offer unconditional love and forgiveness, pets are also healers. Pay attention to the free flow of love they offer; it's an example unsurpassed by humans. No expectations. No conditions. No pressure. Pets offer round-the-clock availability as kindhearted companions.

As human beings, we often guard against our greatest needs. Your walls go up due to past hurts, disappointments, and intrusions, but in recovery you can learn to safely feel all of your feelings, even the uncomfortable ones. If you're ready to move beyond past emotional ruptures, being in a relationship is the best place to work on them. As avoidance and disconnection dissolve, trust and respect grow. Walking through your fears and vulnerabilities with another person will promote deeper contact, healthier bonds, and bona fide love.

Do you have any pets? If so, how do they provide emotional support?

Alex: *I have two cats. They make everything seem okay. They know when I'm in pain. They comfort me.*

Seth: *I used to have dogs and they were pure unconditional love. They were always happy to see me, they were sad to see me*

leave, and they were always by my side. They nourished
me in ways most people can't.

Before going further, let's explore the elements of emotional intimacy, which require trust, transparency, and time. Intimacy takes shape within romantic relationships, close friendships, with family, and of course with pets. But developing deeper connections with emotionally reliable people necessitates a conscious choice to talk and listen effectively, share openly from your heart, and show empathy to your loved one. It's the only path to real intimacy. All of us have a core desire to be fully seen, heard, understood, valued, and respected. The shared experience of seeing and being seen is essential for intimate contact.

Describe a recent example of intimacy in your life.

Alex: *I sat with my grandfather while he was dying. I held his hand and told him I loved him. It was one of the most profound relationships I've had, because he had done things to me that were ruthless, but I learned to forgive him. I had done ruthless things in response, so it was awesome to forgive each other and be there for that very special moment when he died.*

Robert: *Recent conversations I had with a person I'm dating. What made it meaningful was letting him see things in me that that I don't usually tell people.*

Colin: *Being genuine and authentic with friends and family I trust and receiving that support back.*

As we discussed in Chapter Six, attachment theory explains a lot about sex addiction. In his book *Addiction as an Attachment Disorder*, renowned psychologist Philip J. Flores, PhD, states that addiction can be either a "cause or a consequence" of an avoidant attachment style in relationships. He describes addiction as "a condition of isolation which often originates with insecure attachments," adding that "not everyone with inadequate attachment experiences will become addicted, but everyone with an addiction suffers with attachment difficulties."

In sexual compulsivity, your urges increase when the attachment to self-destructive behavior is stronger than your attachment to the caring relationships in your life. Conversely, healing and intimacy occur if the desire for loving, nurturing relationships overpowers the attachment to compulsive sex.

Accept your need for others as a part of your emotional sobriety. Our society values autonomy; the fact that you need others to survive is too often overlooked. Self-sufficiency is widely celebrated, while asking for help is looked down on. When you learn to rely on emotionally reliable people, your early attachment gaps mend, healing bonds form, and your brain forges new intimacy pathways.

So how do you do this? Through twelve-step involvement, group psychotherapy, or volunteering, to name just a few ways. Let's look at another example.

Case Study Nine: Michael's Love Avoidance

"Intimacy has always been a mystery to me," says my client Michael. "In past relationships, I either felt suffocated or searched out women who were unavailable. In both cases, I suffered. I still don't know how to be an adult in relationships."

Michael has been married to his wife Barbara for five years, but he avoids her bids for intimacy. She pursues, and Michael distances.

During his childhood, his parents never seemed happy. Instead of looking to her husband for emotional support, his mother leaned on Michael. Though he found her too needy at times, he enjoyed the attention and the feeling of importance. By the time Michael was a teenager, he felt uneasy about the way his mother confided in him, but he still went along with it. Michael's father was grateful for the arrangement. He felt less pressure to show up, and over the years had several affairs as he steadily distanced himself from his family.

Relationships felt complicated for Michael. In his twenties, he only dated older married women. Unconsciously, he chose impossible relationships that inevitably resulted in heartbreak. Michael got involved with married women because there was a built-in barrier to keep him safely distanced from deeper contact. In some ways, this felt comfortable. Yet in other ways, it left him lonely and feeling deprived. After several failed relationships, he finally went to therapy and started to understand his avoidant pattern.

Michael began to date single women, but as he'd get close to a girlfriend, he'd reach the point where the relationship felt smothering to him. He would then sabotage it through excessive use of porn and escorts—anything to create emotional distance. As the sexual acting out became more frequent, he grew more frustrated. Michael began to see his failures and wanted more intimacy.

When he turned thirty-four, by which point he was married, Michael attended his first SLAA meeting, where a woman named Valerie shared her story.

"My dad leaned on me way too much," she said. "It almost felt incestuous. Don't get me wrong. I liked being a daddy's girl, but I also hated it. When I'm involved with someone, I run away from them. And outside of a relationship, I long for someone to rescue me."

Valerie's story mirrored Michael's, and for the first time, he didn't feel so alone with what he now recognized as the emotional incest from his mother. This mother-son dynamic often results in love avoidant patterns, such as building walls to prevent feeling overwhelmed by others.

He disclosed this newfound information to his wife, and she expressed openness to understand the themes of his past. Barbara was relieved Michael had taken responsibility for avoiding her all these years, but she wanted more. They went to couples therapy, where they finally came to understand each other's intimacy styles. Michael empathized with his wife's loneliness and became less defensive and more compassionate.

Unfortunately, this improvement was too little too late for Barbara, and she asked Michael for a trial separation. Although he had needed to protect himself in the past by distancing from her, the separation was surprisingly excruciating. With the help of their therapist, they decided to continue therapy but minimize contact beyond their appointments. During the ongoing separation, they are reevaluating their wants and desires, and playing the relationship by ear.

Gradually, you'll learn to trust those who choose to be in your corner, and there are many options. Coaches are future focused and action oriented, so they offer a fresh perspective on your quest for a meaningful life. Moving on to a new career, or resuscitating an existing one, is a way to collaborate with someone toward a purposeful goal. Volunteering is another underutilized means of connecting to your community. If you would like to help children, volunteer at a hospital, library, or Big Brothers Big Sisters of America. By showing an open heart to emotionally deprived kids, you can be of service while experiencing a sense of belonging. It's also refreshing to get to know people who are not in recovery to balance out your social circle.

Your prognosis for long-term recovery depends on you building a stronger capacity to give and receive love, so it's essential to understand potential obstacles like love addiction and love avoidance. Keep in mind that these are patterns of *relating*—they're not actually about love.

Love Avoidance and Love Addiction

If you tend to avoid intimacy, you likely fall into an avoidant attachment category. This is a way to feel less overwhelmed or smothered by the other person. A child with a misattuned parent (a caregiver who is emotionally unavailable or preoccupied) learns to deny the need for anything from them, which results in a counter-dependency and long-term difficulty leaning on others. Love avoidance may work in the short term, but inevitably results in profound loneliness. In the most extreme version of love avoidance, the individual becomes emotionally anorexic, hibernating from contact with others.

Love avoidants may:

- Be enmeshed with a parental relationship
- Feel resentment toward others who express needs
- Appear loving, but have difficulty feeling love
- Be repulsed by intimacy
- Feel smothered in close relationships

• Build walls to regulate emotional distance

A love avoidant person suffers behind their emotional walls and struggles with spontaneity and moderation. It feels safer to hide behind rigid structure and rules. If you identify with this, notice when you're coming out from behind those walls and feel more flexible, spontaneous, and even playful. It may take a while for this to develop, but that intention to move toward emotional contact is what counts, and healing will take place if you stay the course.

Love addiction, meanwhile, may bring back memories of Robert Palmer's 1985 megahit "Addicted to Love." But love addiction is not really about love. It's about the fantasy of love, which reveals itself in highly problematic relationships such as emotional affairs. There may be no sexual involvement, just pseudo-intimate sharing and fantasy. In today's world, love addiction often takes place via social media in exchanges that distract from and jeopardize real-life relationships.

When you get caught in the spell of love addiction, you lose yourself and your grip on reality. Fantasy walls you off from the real world, and full-blown love addicts get obsessed with their idealized vision of love as well as a desire to be rescued. Again, love addiction is really about a self-destructive relationship style based on insecure attachment patterns. Love addiction begins at birth when a parent or caregiver is only intermittently emotionally available. The child longs for a consistent loving presence, yet the parent is only available from time to time. In psychologist B.F. Skinner's early research, he found that rats will die if given too much or too little food. On the other hand, feeding a rat intermittently and unpredictably keeps the rat anticipating the next bit of food impatiently and sometimes ravenously. The same goes for humans. Instead of a flow of reliable love, the love addict eagerly waits for some kind of contact with their love object, no matter how big or how small. This generates tremendous levels of anxiety and dysregulation.

The characteristics of love addiction include:
• Having been raised by a neglectful or absent parent
• A desire to be rescued
• Fears of abandonment and intimacy

- Attraction to a love avoidant
- Creating a fantasy of others
- A withdrawal period after fantasy lifts

Keep in mind that there are many versions of love addiction and love avoidance, and these characteristics describe just some of their typical traits. If you were not raised with a secure attachment—and most sex addicts weren't—it's not too late to develop emotionally reliable attachments as adults. Just because there were attachment gaps in your childhood doesn't mean you have to protect yourself with emotional barriers your entire life. Healthy attachment figures are all around you. Pick a person you trust and nurture this loving relationship.

Deconstructing Obsession

Fantasy and obsession is a powerful drug, but eventually it generates internal turbulence. A typical example is found in romantic idealization. When you think about a person day and night, the fantasy feels exciting and pleasurable at first, but soon it becomes all-consuming and torments you. You think you'll feel better by meeting up or getting something from them, but that's the myth. You will long for contact but feel empty and unsatisfied, because the reality can never live up to the fantasy. These issues occur in any obsessive relationship, whether it involves friends, family, or colleagues.

As painful as obsession can be, it does inform you about your desires, and that knowledge is useful. If you're romantically obsessed, you obviously want something from the other person, be it validation, attention, or sex. When not available, this leaves you highly anxious and longing for the idealized person to fulfill your aching desire. You may lean even further toward the idealized person, believing that your happiness and stability depend on what they do. You then feel destabilized and dysregulated. The impossible love has shown up once again.

Longings associated with love addiction originate from a shame belief that you're not enough, and that by establishing contact with another person, you'll feel better. Unfortunately the fantasy is a mirage, but you keep trying to make it real. When you feel destabilized by an obsessive relationship, you'll know it's a mirage because it will feel as though you're losing your mind. On the other hand, when you feel more stable it's likely that the connection you have is the real deal.

The following strategies will help you move beyond obsession, learn about your vulnerable side, and give your mind something else to consider:

1. Think about what you really want from the other person. Once you've identified it, consider ways to bestow that upon yourself. Sense what's missing in you based on what you want from them.

2. Analyze how you can become a giver rather than a taker. Instead of getting stuck wanting, recognize what you have to offer. Once again review the Prayer of St. Francis (see Chapter Four), which celebrates being of service to others and showing a generosity of spirit.

3. Develop a practice to work with your obsessions. Here is a powerful five-step process you can incorporate into a mindfulness or meditation practice:

    - Visualize the other person as happy
    - Ask yourself what your expectation was of this person or relationship?
    - Locate the longing or desire in yourself that sets up this expectation
    - Ask for the willingness to do whatever is necessary to bring about change in your attitude
    - Repeat over and over to yourself: *I accept the other person exactly the way they are at any given moment*

Pursuer-Distancer Dynamic

Another way to refer to love addiction and love avoidance is the *pursuer-distancer dynamic*. We're all pursuers and distancers at some point in our relationships. The pursuer can resemble the love addict, and the distancer appears love avoidant, but these roles are reversed from time to time. One person actively seeks love and attention from their partner, and at other times that same person backs off and needs space. This is actually a way to keep the heat alive and, when necessary, regulate the emotional distance. If not excessive, it creates healthy longing and desire within the relationship. But take a look at your part in the dance to make sure it's not reaching toxic, unmanageable levels.

The pursuer wants more closeness, desires heart-to-heart talks, and can feel rejected when the distancer asks for too much space. The distancer tends to seek emotional distance at times of high stress, considers themselves self-sufficient, and opens up more when they aren't being pursued or criticized by their partner. These are both survival strategies to cope with an insecure attachment. As you stumble and fumble through the world of relationships, you'll get to observe your attachment patterns in action. But hopefully now that you're aware of these emotional pitfalls, you won't let them ruin important emotional connections.

Many years ago, I asked my friend Liz how she and her partner had stayed happily married for twenty-three years. Her answer was simple: "Walks." For all these years they'd walked together more days than not, and this was their time to connect. There were many meaningful conversations on these walks, during which they observed in themselves and each other how and when closeness waxed and waned in the relationship. Communicate, stay connected through good times and bad, and hold the intention to have each other's back. These are the pillars of secure attachment.

Is there a difference between how you used to feel about intimacy and how you feel about it now?

Alex: *I thought intimacy could only happen with a lover. Now I've discovered you can have it with a lot of different people—like friends—and it's possible to be physically intimate with someone and not emotionally intimate with them. I don't have any judgment about that anymore like I used to.*

Colin: *Intimacy was always something that I wanted, but it felt nebulous and elusive. Today, I feel it's more real. I have experiences with it, with friends and people in recovery, and I feel it in a way I never did before recovery.*

Alex illustrates an option for sexual intimacy that may work for some and not others. Having sex with friends or people you meet solely for sexual play falls within the broader parameters of sexual health, but doesn't fit neatly into the realm of an emotionally intimate relationship. Nonetheless, this option may be a part of a long-term recovery if handled thoughtfully.

All of this—the compulsive sex, the emotional longing, the relationship struggles—is about the same thing: love. That feeling of warm personal attachment or deep affection. Intimacy and love are clearly different from the intense, adrenaline-seeking behaviors and relationships you engaged in before, and so your greatest challenge is to lean into the warm, fuzzy feelings with your loved ones. This chart outlines some of the differences between authentic intimacy and pseudo-intimacy:

Authentic Intimacy & Love	Pseudo-Intimacy & Pseudo-Love
Develops after you feel secure.	Tries to create love even though you feel frightened and insecure.
Comes from feeling full.	Always trying to fill an inner void.
Begins with loving yourself–being the person you think you want and desire.	Tries to avoid introspection and always seeks love from that special someone.
Is based on your ability to love and trust yourself and then others.	Seeks sex and romance outside, precisely because you feel empty inside and don't trust yourself or others.
Allows you to be vulnerable and take risks because you feel secure inside.	Is based on a shaky foundation–you feel you must protect yourself.
Grows slowly, like a tree.	Grows fast, as if by magic.
Thrives on time alone.	Is frightened of being alone.
Teaches you to value your own company.	Makes you feel uncomfortable with yourself and in need of someone else.
Flows out.	Caves in.
Creates a deeper sense of yourself the longer you're together.	Creates a loss of self the longer you're together.

Authentic Intimacy & Love	Pseudo-Intimacy & Pseudo-Love
Gets easier as time goes on.	Gets more complicated as time goes on.
Is like rowing across a gentle lake.	Is like being swept down a raging river.
Is satisfied with the partner you have.	Is always looking for more or better.
Teaches that you're responsible for your own feelings.	Expects that you're responsible for the other person's feelings.
Creates life.	Creates drama.

We all want to be deeply understood, accepted fully, and to feel close to others. Now you have the means to deepen these possibilities. As you reveal more of yourself to others, they get the opportunity to love the real you. Otherwise, the status quo of loneliness will continue.

Among your most intimate relationships, what are the most common qualities?

Mario: *Not having secrets. My old mantra was that "if they really knew who I really was, they'd run." Now they know who I am, and yet they're not running.*

Alex: *Brutal honesty—not holding back what we believe—and humor.*

Seth: *A willingness to be open, vulnerable, honest, and nonjudgmental.*

Robert: *Having each other's back.*

Colin: *Acknowledging each other's feelings in a genuine way and without judgment. In other words, unconditional love and support.*

Relying on the Reliable

There are *your people,* and then there's the rest of the world, and it's your job in life to find *your people.* As you gradually enter the intimacy and love pool, recognize that your people are out there. Consider it a lifelong research project. In what relationships do you feel most like yourself today? Who do you most trust? In which relationships do you feel relaxed? Rely on the reliable and stick with these healing relationships.

Whenever I think of unconditional positive regard and unconditional love, I think of my coach Sam and her consistent, reliable presence. She is an endless source of collaboration, perspective, and inspiration. Her presence and ability to believe in me even at times when I couldn't believe in myself has left me feeling less alone and more hopeful in the many challenges I've faced.

Describe a recent time when others have been emotionally reliable for you, and what made it possible for you to receive their love?

Alex: *When my Grandpa died, my best friend was completely there for me. He checked in with me constantly when I was in the middle of the chaos of my family. I don't think it's something that can happen overnight. People have to earn each other's trust, and we had earned it.*

Colin: *The passing of my mother. The only way I was able to get through that experience relatively intact was by checking in with people I trusted and cared about who supported me—my close confidants and friends. The investment in building those relationships over a number of years had already been made.*

How can you be unconditionally loving to others? How can you be of service to someone who needs a shoulder to lean on? Try to accept others for exactly who they are at any given moment. Don't get caught up in the fantasy that they'll suddenly change to fit your needs. Keep in mind that your physical distance from a person isn't a measure of your loving feelings for them. You may want physical or emotional distance from certain individuals from time to time. But it's how you hold the relationship in your heart that counts. You can love an old friend even while he is trapped in addiction. He is simply being himself.

Being a giver of love is often a bold internal shift for recovering sex addicts. As I stated before, addiction is narcissistic, whereas giving of yourself is an act of generosity. Altruism opens your heart, freeing you to move toward gratitude, humility, and openheartedness. The irony is that when you learn to give more, you also receive more. For example, if you sponsor someone in the program, you automatically stay in contact with the fellowship, which in turn bolsters your recovery.

Action Steps:

1. Lean into safe, loving relationships. Become the pursuer rather than the distancer. Who would you like to pursue as a friend or confidant? Consider your options and choose someone you would like to pursue.

2. Be a giver of love even if that's scary. Notice when love shows up in front of you and take note of how it feels. Track loving moments— both giving and receiving love from others.

3. Learn from your pets. They are instinctive teachers of unconditional love, acceptance, and play. Pay attention to their acceptance. Savor it. If you don't have a pet, consider fostering one or volunteering at your local shelter.

4. Take inventory of the most intimate friendships in your life. Write a list of past relationships that have been the most meaningful. Identify their commonalities.

5. Notice when you feel trust and relaxation in relationships. Without these qualities, intimacy does not exist. Be mindful when you're feeling more relaxed with others. Take note of what happens inside you and how it indicates deepening trust.

6. Identify *your people* and cultivate deeper contact through vulnerability and emotional risk-taking. Be the reliable person you would like to find in others. Consider small emotional risks and show up wholeheartedly for relationships, one intimate moment at a time.

Chapter Ten

A 21st Century Take on Codependency and Boundaries

Compassionate people ask for what they need. They say no when they need to, and when they say yes, they mean it. They're compassionate because their boundaries keep them out of resentment.
—Brené Brown

We are all codependent in one way or another. But if your codependency gets out of control, you lose your emotional sobriety and become vulnerable to relapse. Focusing exclusively on another person, while generous, often results in personal neglect and takes attention away from your recovery. What is often discovered in codependents who engage in compulsive sexual behavior is a childhood pattern of attachment trauma—a disrupted bond between child and parent that manifests as abuse, neglect, or chronic misattunement.

Growing up in a neglectful or abusive home, you go into survival mode. In order to navigate the lack of nurturing, you may have become a pleaser, with difficulty saying no. This matured into a disproportionate need to be liked, which evolved into a lifelong pattern. If it's not possible to say no, boundaries become blurry and are often crossed. As a result, your nervous system is constantly at risk of dysregulation, an emotional rollercoaster. Because your environment was chaotic and unpredictable you tried to control your surroundings, and that left you feeling out of control as well. This is the tip of the iceberg of extreme codependency.

To avoid losing yourself in a relationship, you need to set effective limits. Relational boundaries help establish where your interests end and the other person's begin. You might consider them rules for how you treat each other that are vital to your well-being and the well-being of your relationships.

Creating boundaries provides you with choices you lacked as a child. For example, if you had a parent who was overinvolved in your life, their behavior may have triggered you to act out in the past, and can possibly cause a relapse now. If you don't communicate directly and honestly with them, resentment will build, and before you know it you'll be vulnerable to acting out again. On the other hand, if you learn to say no to them, the hostility you hold will be minimal; you'll have steered away from potential problems. By fine-tuning your boundaries, you'll establish trust with those who respect your limits.

To establish your boundaries, reflect back on your relationships. From childhood on, your boundaries were likely invaded or ignored. Now comes the time to scrutinize and reclaim your boundaries. As you take inventory of past and current relationship experiences, identify how your survival strategies protected you yet ultimately left you lonely and resentful. Ideally, you'll recognize when you felt nourished and when you felt depleted. Most importantly, you'll clearly understand the lasting benefits of establishing boundaries that are co-created and adopted with people you can count on.

When you were acting out sexually, your physical, sexual, and emotional boundaries were blurry at best. Now it's time to clarify them one relationship at a time. This can be a painstaking process, but will help you to determine which relationships to cultivate, limit, or eliminate entirely.

I always knew my family was good, despite having a lot of problems. Deep down we loved each other, but we didn't know how to express it, and as a result we held rigid boundaries, not letting anyone get too close. I took on the hero role and wanted to fix everyone who was suffering, especially my mother. I grew into a "needless/wantless" kid who was exceptionally self-reliant. Since I didn't trust that anyone in my family would know how to take care of me, I became a heat-seeking missile that looked for validation and love outside the family. Eventually this evolved into self-destructive behaviors, such as extreme perfectionism and problematic sexual choices.

The intertwined nature of attachment trauma and codependency revealed itself in my desperate urge to save or be saved by others. Any life event that is too much to process at the time qualifies as trauma. My outward focus appeared to be on others' well-being, but underneath it all I hoped that someone would take me away from my own loneliness and pain. Eventually it became crystal clear that my healing path was solely up to me.

Your current relationship challenges, such as resentments, communication breakdowns, and emotional hurts, might seem like recent issues, but a history of abandonment, abuse, or neglect would suggest otherwise. And the debilitating nature of codependency is such that it may also result in love addiction, martyrdom, anxiety, depression, and rage. If you chronically blame others for your pain, the victim role isolates you even further.

Codependency is an innocent attempt to feel better during emotional neglect, so it's best not to judge yourself too harshly. That said, it's important to understand this coping strategy. Here are typical ways you've likely used codependency to protect yourself:

Black-and-White Thinking

All-or-nothing, rule-based approaches feel safer to codependents. This rigid way of viewing yourself and others results in profound loneliness and unexpressed anger, traits that turn others off and keep you walled in. Pay attention to your black-and-white thinking, and keep a daily log to track examples. Build awareness, curiosity, and a nonjudgmental perspective. Write down a contrary action for each example of black-and-white thinking and develop more flexible ways to approach these situations or relationships.

Personalization

The codependent takes everything personally because they have an out-of-proportion need to be liked, as well as a fear of abandonment. They interpret everything as being about them, which builds a wall of rage and defensiveness. Give yourself permission, at least initially, to experience your reaction, knowing it's a protective instinct. Write down examples of personalization in an effort to notice how often and with whom the incidents occur. Get out of your own head and move toward a less narcissistic position by being honest with yourself and others about taking things so personally. The first of the Twelve Steps suggests you acknowledge the problem. Not taking things personally is a necessary pillar of life contentment.

Intellectualization

Obsessive overanalysis, sometimes referred to as intellectualization, results in severe anxiety and isolation. It's a wall. Critical thinking is revered in our culture, but it often leads to unintended distancing from others. If you live in your head most of the time, you often override your body and spirit. The overanalyzer has trouble identifying emotions and sensations. The healing direction is to help all parts of you fall into balance. Build somatic awareness, checking in with your body to know what's happening from the neck down. By working with a somatically trained therapist or other mindfulness professional, the intellectualizer can tune the brain and body to be in harmony, and thus experience more vulnerability, as well as deeper relationships.

Catastrophizing

When you find yourself obsessing about something bad happening in the future, you're catastrophizing. This usually results from the anxiety, trauma, or addiction that you were exposed to as a kid. You learned then to expect the worst. Disappointment was a constant, and as a result you're always waiting for the other shoe to drop. Obsessing over worst-case scenarios takes you into the future rather than leaving you in the moment. When you find yourself catastrophizing (or future-tripping), come back to the here and now through such somatic tools as grounding, orienting, and mindful breathing. It's also soothing to think about people in your life who are emotionally reliable. Broken relationships are sources of deep pain, suffering, and anxiety, so lean into loving, comforting relationships, and eventually catastrophizing will subside.

When you're stuck in codependent, unproductive relationships, they often feel comfortable and familiar, making it difficult to imagine more boundaried relationships. You may not know any other way of relating. If walking on eggshells has been your norm since childhood, you probably don't even realize you're doing it. Profound suffering in relationships is the wake-up call to examine your part in them. Rawly Glass, a renowned clinical social worker, calls codependency a "painful" dependence on anything outside of yourself. But when you count on people who are emotionally reliable, trust grows and codependency subsides.

For Terry Kellogg, a family systems pioneer, the problem in codependency isn't the relationship with the other person—it's the absence of a relationship with yourself. When you put all of your focus on another person, you neglect your own needs. Your suffering has been based on a hollowness left over from past wounds. Therefore, healing has to take shape from within—not by changing or manipulating others.

Codependency 101

Here are the four types of codependency identified by the twelve-step programs of Al-Anon and Co-Dependents Anonymous, and refined by family systems experts through the years:

- Fixing   • Enabling
- Rescuing   • Caretaking

Fixing is a tactic to take away someone else's pain. Most of the time it occurs when the fixer can't tolerate another person's suffering. Fixing doesn't allow the other person to experience themselves as fully competent, and keeps them in an inferior position. So while fixing may seem generous, it's actually self-centered and one-sided.

Rescuing is best illustrated by the story of the knight in shining armor, in which a heroic figure arrives to save a helpless person in distress. The fallacy is in thinking the rescuer can always swoop in to make everything better for the distressed person and they will live happily ever after. Many of you grew up with media content that perpetuated this fantasy; it provided a way to escape your chaotic childhood. Kids don't have the tools to navigate trauma, but now you can act as your own knight in shining armor by becoming the capable, competent person you truly are.

Enabling refers to inadvertently colluding in or supporting the addict's behavior. The enabler might set a boundary, claiming for example that they'll divorce the sex addict if they don't stop having affairs by a certain date. When they don't follow through on this threat, not only are they disempowering themselves, they are also communicating to the sex addict that their boundaries aren't real. Remaining silent about the addict's sexual acting out is another form of enabling.

Caretaking is a problem rooted in the loved one's insecurity, poor boundaries, and need for control, which results in high levels of stress and depletion. You lose yourself by putting all of your energy into your loved one, and the relationship is out of balance. Care*giving,* on the other hand, involves clear boundaries and a balanced relationship with others. You're providing care to your loved one but also taking good care of yourself. In contrast to caretaking, where you try to dominate everything, caregiving comes from your generosity of spirit and unconditional love.

Codependent traits exist in all of us, but the codependent part of you likely overfunctions in an attempt to feel better or possibly feel less. It takes time and perseverance to break these patterns, but through self-awareness and clear-cut boundaries, you can seek more balanced, mutually respectful relationships originating in love.

Codependency makes you vulnerable to relapse if not addressed. How would you describe codependency in your relationships, and how have you been working on it?

Alex: *The most codependent relationship I've ever had was with my mom. She tried to get me to be her husband and father and son all at once. It was a really twisted relationship. I had to give her what she wanted emotionally in order to get what I wanted financially. Since going to medical school, I've cut that off and am completely self-sufficient. I don't talk about money with her and try not to get in situations where I'm around her for extended periods of time.*

Seth: *I've addressed it through therapy and by going to Al-Anon meetings. I'm learning about detachment and how I get caught up with others in unhealthy ways.*

Mario: *It mostly manifested in me wanting to control the other person. Now it's about learning to accept that the other person is not an appendage.*

Robert: *Trying to be there for the other person without losing myself. Boundaries always have to be for myself and never against somebody else.*

Colin: *When I start putting too much focus on the other person and basing my well-being on their needs or reactions. I know I'm getting into a codependent dynamic when I become agitated. Another sign of codependency is when there's something in my life I'm avoiding by putting my focus on another person. I have to ask myself, "What part of my life do I not want to deal with?" and begin using the tools to work on that.*

Susan: *Before recovery, I would take people hostage and want them to do everything for me, and I would do everything for them. There were no boundaries. In recovery, my boundaries are stronger, and because of all the writing and step work I have more awareness of who I am, what I want, and how to verbalize that. A lot of my codependency*

*was from not knowing who I was or what I wanted. I
would glom on to people and become a chameleon to be
liked by them. I would find people who needed more help
than I did and try to help them, instead of helping myself.*

Blurry Boundaries

Codependency thrives on a lack of personal, sexual, and emotional boundaries. But before constructing new and effective boundaries, it's essential to recognize the poor boundaries that fostered your out-of-control sexual behavior. Here's a list of blurry sexual boundaries:
- Intrigue with a partnered person
- Meeting sexual partners in a twelve-step program
- Sharing sexual history on a first date
- Neglecting your wants and desires in order to be liked
- Allowing others to violate your sexual boundaries
- Touching someone without their consent

Clear-cut boundaries will make your life simpler, but require a willingness to identify and practice them. Be humble, and ask a sponsor, therapist, or coach for help in applying your boundaries. Make a commitment to establish clarity and integrity in all your relationships.

When you negotiate boundaries with a loved one, it paves the way for mutual respect. Not all friends and family will choose to participate in this intimate process, but either way, you always get to refine boundaries from your perspective. Sometimes others will surprise you and join in later once they see how determined you are to clarify what you want and don't want. Because intimacy isn't fully possible without trust and respect, boundaries are a prerequisite to sustaining satisfying, loving relationships.

Clear-Cut Boundaries

Boundaries can be classified according to the following four categories adapted from Pia Mellody:

1. ***Physical Boundaries:*** To regulate the physical distance between yourself and others, clarify how much or how little touch you like. This may sound simple, but it's often forgotten. You ought to respect other people's personal boundaries too. If someone gets tearful in a twelve-step meeting, for example, others in the group may want to place a hand on their knee or give the person crying a hug. This is presumptuous behavior. You don't know if the person wants space, or is triggered by unsolicited physical contact. Usually in a case like this, the person who wants to initiate touch is expressing their own difficulty tolerating the emotion being expressed, and reaches out to console the other person without considering their own codependent tendencies. Approach physical contact with caution and respect. It's always best to ask first.

2. ***Sexual Boundaries:*** Decide when, where, and how you'll invite sexual contact of any kind. Also, start an honest conversation with a partner about mutual sexual boundaries. By sharing these parameters, mutual respect and trust will grow.

3. ***Emotional Boundaries:*** Regulate your feelings by choosing the right amount of emotional distance for you. This boundary reminds you that you always have emotional wants and desires. Not everyone will be available at the right time or at the right emotional temperature, but don't take this personally. Everyone has their own way of communicating, which is rooted in their emotional history. It's not necessarily about you.

4. ***Intellectual Boundaries:*** You have your own beliefs and opinions, and you can express them as you wish, knowing that you're accountable for the consequences. All of your thoughts and ideas are a part of who you are, and expressing yourself assertively allows others to clearly understand your intentions.

Because your experience with boundaries (and sexual boundaries in particular) has been loose in the past, it will take time to establish new ones. Here are some tangible examples of how your boundaries may be tested, and how you might respond:

- When you feel offended by someone, it's okay to confront them or choose not to, but always process your feelings with a trusted confidant. Write a resentment inventory, or take a few minutes to meditate before proceeding.
- If the other person has a habit of violating boundaries, it's time to ask them to stop and to let them know the consequence of further boundary violations.
- Say no when you want to say no. Don't be wishy-washy. Remember that by issuing a firm *no*, you'll enjoy more sureness when you decide to say *yes*.
- If you're not clear about your boundary in the moment, it's helpful to say maybe and let them know you'll get back to them. There's no need to commit to an exact answer when you're feeling unsure.
- If the other person doesn't understand or respect the word *no*, it's time to set limits or possibly end the relationship.

Let's see how a lack of boundaries can manifest at a very young age and haunt a person well into their adult life—or indefinitely—if not addressed.

Case Study Ten: Sophia's Lack of Boundaries

Sophia was eight years old when her favorite cousin Eli molested her. He was fifteen, nearly twice her age, and Sophia idolized him. She never wanted to disappoint him in any way. Eli had been sexually abused as a young child by a teenage girl who babysat him, and his sexual advances toward Sophia reenacted his own abuse. Sophia was conflicted. On the one hand, she loved the attention from her cousin. On the other hand, it felt wrong. She didn't tell anyone about the secret nighttime visits from Eli. Sophia's abuse weighed on her for years, and when puberty arrived she began to masturbate compulsively to self-soothe.

"Once I knew how to make myself climax, I couldn't stop. I did it multiple times a day, to the point where I would injure myself," she says.

"I realized as an adult this was my way to feel better, but at the time it was an urge that I couldn't stop."

Soon, Sophia began to experiment sexually with any willing partner, and saw life through a highly sexualized lens. As time went on, she realized she was more attracted to girls, and she knew how to lure them into her bedroom as "friends with benefits." It was a game of seduction.

"I became ravenous," Sophia says. "I wanted to see how far they would let me go, and I wanted the warmth of another body. I wondered, how many girls will play around with me if I invite them into my bed? I got quite good at this game, but unfortunately I also developed a reputation as a slut."

From the time Eli molested her, Sophia had poor boundaries. She never learned how to say no, and would say yes even when she wanted to say no. Sophia had a strong desire to be liked by everyone, at all times, and never wanted to disappoint others. Her inability to say no was rooted in the cousin incest. She never understood how to protect herself or identify what she truly wanted.

After growing progressively more miserable, Sophia went to therapy during her junior year of high school. The therapist said, "It's not your fault. It's never been your fault. You're a survivor. And you're going to get through this." Immediately, Sophia felt less alone, and came to understand that sexual abuse was a part of her family legacy she wanted to break.

Sophia was a serial dater through her late teens and twenties, and always had challenges with trust and vulnerability. At twenty-nine, she went through a painful breakup, and after that she found a somatically trained therapist who specialized in sexual abuse. Sophia had been a self-sufficient young woman who was emotionally isolated. She never got too close to anyone; tantrums, crying spells, and blaming her partners had always been the norm.

"I finally understood that I was angry, hurt, and disappointed with Eli," Sophia says. "But I was terrified to be honest with him. I needed to release my stored memories with someone emotionally dependable like my therapist. We looked at my patterns with sex and intimacy, and I had self-compassion for the part of me that was terrified to trust again.

"As I became more aware of my moodiness and my emotional reactivity, my nervous system relaxed. I know I have a long way to go, but I do know one thing—I want loving relationships in my life, and it's going to take time to accept this possibility."

Here are some practical strategies for establishing healthier boundaries:

1. Stop caretaking others. You may have a habit of taking care of the person crossing your boundaries. Bite your tongue and choose not to take care of them; remind yourself that you're not responsible for their feelings.

2. Don't let yourself be used anymore. As a child, you may have experienced boundary intrusion and felt afraid to say no. As a result, you felt shame and hopelessness. Don't fall in the quicksand of shame. Be patient with yourself as you develop new habits with every boundary you set.

3. Use anger safely and productively. It lets you know that something is not right. Listen to this call-to-action as a clue to set new boundaries. Boundaries bring up an abundance of complicated feelings, but utilizing them results in self-respect.

4. When you set new boundaries in old relationships, you'll be tested. Make sure you're prepared to hold your boundary when you set it. Be clear and concise. Keep in mind that those who choose to be in a relationship with you will want to work things out.

5. Boundaries need to be verbally and behaviorally congruent. As you identify the emotionally reliable people in your life, you will need to be more emotionally reliable too. Being consistent with your thoughts, feelings, and actions is a measure of emotional sobriety and clear boundaries.

6. You determine when you feel prepared to set a boundary. There's no timeline. But it will lighten the burden you feel to set standards for how and when you share your time, energy, and love.

7. Before you set a boundary, it's always helpful to run it by someone for a reality check. You'll feel more confident in your decision afterward. Swim with those dolphins who respect and encourage you. Surround yourself with wise, loving people who provide perspective as you navigate these choppy seas.

8. One primary reason for boundaries is to define and strengthen your relationships. Reconfiguring relationships takes time and patience, and clarifies who your true dolphins are. Who do you really want in your pod?

Describe boundaries in your life and your recovery today.

Alex: *I don't have unprotected sex—I make that very clear. And I'm becoming more boundaried about my time. If somebody wants to do something and I know it's going to stress me out, I say no.*

Mario: *I've established emotional boundaries, having learned in the professional arena not to get sucked into the drama that's out there. I'm able to see it for what it is, watching instead of falling into it.*

Robert: *I speak up for myself. I say when I'm feeling uncomfortable. I always look at what's good for me and what is not. Sexually, I go with what feels comfortable and take it more seriously when something isn't quite right.*

Colin: *I came from a household where there weren't many boundaries, and the boundaries we had were fused, meshed, loose, vague, and just not respected. I didn't know what they were, or how to maintain them if I did. What I've learned in recovery is that my boundaries are my responsibility. I have to state them in a way that's compassionate and neutral, and not blow the other person out of the water. My boundaries are what works and doesn't work for me. I can't assume the other person is going to figure that out.*

Anger and Saying No

Because anger is typically labeled as a negative emotion, you might have overlooked its value as a boundary setter. It doesn't have to occur at high-decibel levels, and should be recognized as a need to express something that would otherwise get bottled up. Anger can bring you closer to others when shared directly, honestly, and clearly. Within anger there can be love and wisdom, especially when you're able to express it without being vindictive or mean. Trusted loved ones will generally accept and even respect anger that is expressed in nonreactive ways, and as a result, the relationship will be more genuine.

By the same token, once you develop a capacity to say *yes, no,* or *maybe* in your relationships, you clarify for others exactly where you stand. Expressing previously unexpressed emotions strengthens your boundaries and sets the stage for more meaningful contact.

This all requires practice, especially if you have a strong need to be liked and are unaccustomed to disappointing others. Saying *no* when you clearly want to say no may frustrate people, but the more important thing is your self-respect, and a person who truly cares will eventually come to understand that.

Just as unexpressed anger and resentment may come out through out-of-control sexual behavior, shame can cause your compulsivity to grow. If you carry the shame belief that sex is bad, you'll be more likely to partake in it in secretive, unhealthy ways. The more unconditionally accepting of yourself you are, the more emotionally sober you'll feel. So keep this in mind—unexpressed anger and cumulative shame create vulnerability to poor boundaries, problematic behavior, and possible relapse.

What is your greatest challenge with boundaries today?

Mario:	*There are still times when I forget that other people are not just appendages of mine.*

Seth:	*When other people don't respect my boundaries, I get angry and reactive in certain ways.*

Alex:	*It's hard when I disappoint somebody and they're upset with me. My mom will say really awful things if she doesn't get what she wants, and that's very painful. My work is to*

go through the pain without reacting, which is what she
wants. It's really hard. There's no easy way to do it. I go
through the pain of displeasing a person, displeasing myself,
and all the emotions that go into saying no.

What would your life look like without codependency and blurry boundaries? Emotional sobriety? Freedom? Love and intimacy? This chapter of your sexual recovery journey requires tremendous endurance and determination, but it's worth it to foster loving, respectful connections.

Action Steps:
1. Codependency is a hidden form of suffering that creates greater vulnerability to relapse. Track your codependent behavior. Journal about how it served you in the past, then write out contrary actions for each identified trait.
2. Compulsive sex and codependency both derive from relational traumas such as abandonment, enmeshment, abuse, and neglect. Consider healing your trauma through somatic therapy, group therapy, or residential workshops.
3. Clear-cut boundaries define where you end and the other person begins. Regulating the emotional distance in your relationships is a vital part of recovery. Recognize how and why you regulate distance, and with whom.
4. Unexpressed anger puts you at risk of acting out in one form or another. But anger is an ally that lets you know when something is unacceptable to you. Notice times when you get angry, and consider ways to safely and productively express it to others.
5. Boundaries begin by determining when you want to say yes, no, or maybe to a request. If you say no, you'll save energy for things you actually want to do. Keep track of your responses to requests for your time and energy. Notice when you say *yes*, yet really want to say maybe or no.

6. Identify your dolphins—especially those who are receptive to your boundaries. By relying on emotionally reliable people, you'll build trust with those who understand and respect your recovery.

Chapter Eleven

Meaning, Purpose, and Legacy

Love is our true destiny. We do not find the meaning of
life by ourselves alone—we find it with one another.
—Thomas Merton

Spirituality, as I've mentioned before, is "whatever gives your life meaning." You have the freedom to find it through your own heart rather than as others define it. A spiritual experience can take many forms—the simple enjoyment of an afternoon with a beloved pet, or on a hike through nature. Meaning and purpose in recovery tend to coalesce around big-ticket items like forgiveness, getting in touch with a Universal Power, and considering your legacy. Sex addiction took you far away from yourself. By reclaiming your passions, values, and goals, you'll feel more true to yourself as you search for purpose and meaning on your recovery path.

Spirituality vs. Religion

I grew up in a liberal Jewish home in South Jersey where it was understood that my brothers and I would attend Hebrew school with the eventual goal of getting bar mitzvahed. This felt isolating to me.

Most of my neighborhood friends were not Jewish, and though I would have preferred to hang out with them after school, I was instead whisked away to synagogue to learn a language that seemed useless and obscure.

In retrospect, I realize that my parents' goal wasn't so much for us to learn Hebrew or strictly adhere to an organized religion. They rather wanted us to develop core values and community. Today, I hold many of the same principles that were instilled in me then as a child—social justice, universal human rights, and altruism. Although the bar mitzvah has long faded from memory, I do remember my parents' pride as I participated in a ritual neither of them had had the opportunity to experience. It was a priceless investment to establish my core values within the spiritual community of that era.

Another cornerstone of my Jewish upbringing was the encouragement to ask questions. Our rabbi's sermons emphasized that there are always more questions than answers in life, which I still find liberating as a recovering perfectionist who always wanted specific solutions to my problems. As I mentioned in Chapter Seven, a few years ago I saw a documentary about Orthodox rabbis in Jerusalem who congregate every day to heatedly debate the spiritual questions and dilemmas they face as religious leaders. Their exchanges were so animated—their passions fueled by the investigation of possibilities—despite no specific answers or outcomes being available. As with any productive debate, participants grew more enthusiastic in the face of a challenge, and to me this palpable image demonstrated vitality in the midst of an ancient city wrought with religious conflict. Their purpose was not to one-up each other or arrive at a unanimous conclusion. It was about connection and community.

Religion is typically practiced in a place of worship through the close study of a sacred text. The Torah, the Bible, and the Koran each provide structure to their followers, and these religious traditions have been handed down through the generations and practiced worldwide. Both of my parents grew up in Brooklyn, New York, which has a vibrant Jewish culture celebrated by comedians like Jerry Seinfeld and many others for its bustling delis, hot bagels, and Yiddish expressions. All four of my grandparents were fluent in Yiddish. It will always be a part of my heritage, and though nowadays I only throw around select phrases on occasion, their language and culture live on as a part of my spirituality. When I think about a hot knish, or a corned beef sandwich, it puts a smile on my face. I love sharing these memories because they're a part of my identity.

My background illustrates how organized religion overlaps with cultural identity and spirituality. Sometimes religion and culture interweave; sometimes they're distinctly separate. Along these lines, twelve-step programs follow spiritual traditions but are intended to be free of religious dogma. How then might you choose to consider a Higher Power or traverse a spiritual path?

Unfortunately, not all religions are open-minded. Many of them discourage people from wandering outside their rigid doctrine. There's also an epidemic of religious trauma in the world—deep wounds caused by harsh restrictions, full-blown abuse, and exile from religious communities and leaders.

I believe most if not all addicts have experienced some type of trauma in their past. It may have been coming out as an LGBT person, having an abortion, or doing drugs that resulted in harsh disapproval or estrangement—families fractured, couples separated, and children given ultimatums. This adds a layer of loneliness, conflict, and despair to the search for meaning. Each of you has the right to choose what gives your life purpose; nobody can interfere with your soul-searching. If you've been harmed by a religious community, seek help from a licensed psychotherapist who specializes in religious trauma and understands the intricacies of those complicated wounds.

Sex addiction recovery is frequently misunderstood by families, friends, and communities at large. A stigma still surrounds it. Educating your loved ones on this issue can be a mutually healing experience if they are openhearted enough to understand that it's not about the sex. If they are not open to discussion, lean into the love wherever it exists for you, like with your *family of choice*. Sit down with a qualified family therapist as well, but make sure they are trained to understand your version of trauma and brokenheartedness as you steer toward healing.

Millions of people have found help and hope in the twelve-step programs, which are also considered spiritual groups. When Alcoholics

Anonymous was founded in 1935, it was born out of a need for individuals addicted to alcohol to break out of isolation. This holds true for all self-medicating behaviors, including compulsive sex. Moving from isolation to connection has been a vital part of my own healing and was a catalyst for writing this book. It's not about the sex—it's about giving and receiving love, and developing deeper personal connections. Relationships are hard work, but they're also the only way to mend your broken heart and experience true intimacy.

In twelve-step rooms you're told to take what you like and leave the rest. You may gravitate toward certain people and be put off by others. The program is meant to offer spiritual suggestions, not a rigid system. If you hear too much dogmatic talk, that's probably just how some individual is choosing to work their program—not an interpretation for you or an insistence that you do it their way. And there are always other meetings, both in-person and online, that you can find. The Twelve Steps offer a spiritual direction for emotional and sexual sobriety through which you can find what gives your life meaning.

Universal Energy

One of the most important steps involves the development of a relationship with a power greater than ourselves. This moves you beyond self-centeredness and isolation, toward other-centeredness and intimacy. Whether it's a relationship with God, a Higher Power, a power greater than yourself, or a Universal Power is irrelevant. You may be atheist or agnostic. However you identify, the most important thing to consider is meaningful connection to the world around you. Out-of-control sexual behavior is a narcissistic, selfish experience; a vital element of healing is the exploration of your life purpose and meaning. It's up to you how you'll define Universal Energy; you can use any activity or relationship as a starting point. Again, there's no right or wrong approach—it's simply an opportunity to consider the wisdom and perspective available to you.

What gives your recovery spiritual meaning today?

Colin: *Not isolating. Not having to carry the burden alone. Connecting through prayer and meditation. Being of service to others, which has expanded into a new career path.*

Susan: *Helping others; because of my own background, I'm especially qualified to educate people about porn and prostitution. I find meaning by supporting people as they work the steps. I feel like that's my higher purpose. I came into recovery and got free, and then helped others get free.*

Seth: *Doing things I enjoy, like hiking, playing guitar, and my therapy work. Being with my significant other. Connecting with my kids.*

Alex: *I'm entering a profession where I help people, so that's a big one. But I think what I want to do more is to give kindness to others all the time. Buddhist meditation is also a big part of my life. It opens doors and gives me clarity.*

Mario: *Participating in, instead of watching, my life.*

What is a spiritual life? Is it reserved for some and not others? You all have a spiritual life inside you, available if you choose to explore it. Opening your heart and your mind to examine what matters most to you is a door to a spiritual life. Your spirit may have been put on hold during a chaotic childhood or while in active addiction, but it's always available to rekindle.

Let's look at an example of a late spiritual awakening from a person who hardly recognized himself before it occurred.

Case Study Eleven: Stuart's Sense of Purpose and Spirituality

Stuart's parents were devout Christians who organized their lives around their church. Out of obligation, he went along with them, but he knew from an early age that its dogma would never resonate.

"I've never been a believer," Stuart says. "My parents dragged me along with them, but it never made any sense to me."

Santa Claus, the Easter Bunny, and holiday gifts were welcome. But the rest was alien to him.

By the time he was an adult, Stuart prided himself on being agnostic. He didn't get argumentative with his parents, but still felt like an outsider in the family. Stuart's older sister and younger brother went along with their parents and chose to raise their families in accordance with the Christian faith. Stuart, meanwhile, held divergent political views and moved to a large, culturally liberal city.

In his late twenties, Stuart met Megan, and they married shortly thereafter. They had two daughters. Stuart enjoyed a successful career as an electrical engineer while Megan worked as a high school teacher. On the outside, everything looked great. Yet on the inside, Stuart had a vague feeling of dissatisfaction. When he turned forty, he began reevaluating his life choices.

Stuart and his friend Bob trained for and completed a triathlon together, an exhilarating bonding experience, and shortly thereafter Bob invited Stuart to celebrate by taking ecstasy. In the past, they'd only drank beers together. This was the first time drugs were added to the mix. Megan was out of town with the girls, so Stuart threw caution to the wind and said okay. He'd never felt anything like it before. Soon, these middle-aged friends were flirting with younger women at a local bar. Not only did this seem out of character for Stuart, he also risked being seen by someone in their community. Before he knew it, Stuart was hooking up with one of the women. It felt like floodgates had opened.

Taking ecstasy was the gateway for Stuart to hook up regularly with women at bars, get erotic massages, and eventually hire escorts. Part of him knew this was a midlife crisis, and that the sex and ecstasy were an escape. Whether it was the profound loneliness in his childhood, or an unexplored trail of pain in his adult life that did it, he was becoming someone he didn't recognize. The ecstasy had become a door to his shadow side.

For the next eighteen months, Stuart acted out sexually at least once a week, lying to both Megan and his boss. He knew he was playing with fire and could lose his marriage, children, and his career. One day Megan stumbled upon an email from an escort who wanted to set up a date with Stuart. She was in disbelief, but now his distancing made more sense to her.

They had communicated well in the past, so when Megan confronted Stuart, he came clean about his sexual compulsion and the ecstasy use. Megan felt terribly hurt and wanted to see a couples therapist to work things out. After getting a referral from a friend who had been healing from infidelities, they attended their first session and experienced both relief and hope. They knew it was going to be a long road, but were invested in learning about themselves and one another.

After six months of therapy, as well as life transition coaching, Stuart joined a men's group with a focus on recovery from infidelities and compulsive sex. He began to see all of these events as an opportunity to explore his spiritual side. Although religion was not on his radar, finding meaning and purpose was a priority. He had never examined what mattered most to him, but came to realize that his family and friends were paramount. Until now, he had felt muted on the inside, which left him highly vulnerable to stepping out on his marriage.

With the help of therapy and his coach, Stuart identified love, contribution, and connection as his highest core values, and he found himself realigning with his true self. Although he recognizes that he has a long way to go, Stuart feels awakened at this midway point in his life. By realigning his priorities with his passions, he understands what matters most to him, and as a result has become less vulnerable to future relapse.

How would you describe your spiritual life today?

Mario: *I have a Higher Power. It's a private relationship that doesn't go through a church, but there is a dialogue. I try to connect in a consistent way through some form of prayer, or by experiencing the beauty in nature, art, and music.*

Seth: *Mindfulness. Trying to stay in the moment. I do slip into the past or future sometimes, but I try to reel myself back.*

Colin: *Words cannot begin to describe it. It's such a 180 from
where I was five years ago and for the first thirty-five
years of my life, when spirituality was nonexistent. I don't
think of my spiritual life now as separate from the other
parts of my life. They are one and the same, including
prayer, connecting with others, and doing service work in
the program.*

Once again, I highly recommend some type of morning tone-setter
for yourself. As you become more interested in what your inner world is
communicating, listen to the spiritual possibilities that emerge. It may
include prayer, meditation, journaling, or reading a passage from an
inspirational book. But don't limit yourself to what others do or say.
Follow your rhythm and find time each day. One thing I do before
closing my eyes for meditation each morning is to think of people
I know who are suffering in some way. It's my way to hold them in my
heart and acknowledge the gratitude I have for the richness of my life.

Spirituality thrives on love, kindness, beauty, and compassion. If
you're inclined to cultivate these qualities, try the following exercise:

- List all the sources of love in your life today.
- List all the sources of beauty in your life today.
- List all the sources of kindness in your life today.
- List all the sources of compassion in your life today.

By paying attention to your inner life, you remind yourself that these
are resources to feel more grounded and relaxed. Opening your heart to
these sources of contentment also opens a wider channel for forgiveness
and appreciation.

For many, the exploration of a Higher Power, Universal Energy, or
God is a strange and foreign task, because there's no scientific evidence
to back it up. Be curious about your skepticism, doubt, and uncertainty,
but stay open-minded to the search for meaning.

When Susan left the sex trade, she immersed herself in a twelve-
step program and in being of service. She found purpose in taking
commitments at meetings and sponsoring other women, while at the

same time enjoying time with friends and her passions. Susan found freedom through working the steps and establishing a brand new relationship with her Higher Power. You will have as many questions as you have answers, but if you can become more comfortable with uncertainty, you're already on your way to a spiritual journey.

If you can't develop a relationship with a Higher Power, you might instead pursue the notion of a "power greater than yourself," as the Twelve Steps suggest. Many newcomers consider the twelve-step fellowship, nature, or a beloved pet to represent Universal Energy. Because other-centeredness tends to bring about deeper contact and healing, I suggest you be creative with this soul-searching process, knowing that these spiritual concepts will evolve over time.

The first three steps of the Twelve Steps focus on developing a relationship with a Higher Power. How would you describe your relationship with a Higher Power today?

Colin: *It's personal. It's conscious. It's active. It has challenges. It's loving. It's nurturing. It's supportive. It's fun. It's the most important aspect of my life. Without that relationship the rest of my life doesn't work.*

Susan: *It's one of trust and relaxation. God is not the most optimal word. Higher Power isn't either. It's more like the energy of the world. The energy of the universe.*

Robert: *Today my relationship with my Higher Power is a much closer, simpler relationship. I used to perceive a Higher Power at a great distance. Now I'm able to see it in small things, like nature.*

Mario: *Before, it was definitely a scolding, disapproving, never happy with me Higher Power. Now I know that's not it.*

Seth: *I've developed a concept of a Higher Power that really works in my recovery. But I still have resistance to reaching out to it. I don't tap into it as often as I feel I could or maybe even should.*

Alex: *Knowing I'm not in charge is a big thing for me. I know*
                 there's something out there. I know there's a God. When
                 I'm not in charge, it makes life a little bit easier.

Purpose and Direction

You might feel eager sometimes to move into action before you've established direction or purpose. For example, you want to start dating but haven't given yourself time and space to come up with a safe dating plan. The first step is to slow down and listen to your unique rhythm. What matters most to you about dating again? Rather than moving immediately into action, consider how you would like to go about this differently at this point in your recovery. If you have a coach, use them as a sounding board to prepare you for a thoughtful entry back into the dating world.

Eliminating out-of-control sexual behaviors frees up energy to reevaluate what matters most to you. Return to core values and purposeful intentions, and design a mission statement now that the fog of compulsive sex has lifted.

A mission statement reflects who you are and what you want to give to others. It presents your essence and purpose, and creates direction for action steps. A mission statement may be a sentence or two, or perhaps longer. Know that it can be revised over time. Be sure to include your core values, qualities, and strengths. Here is one way to construct a mission statement:

Mission Statement = Actions + Values + Receivers
- Actions: Verbs describing where you choose to focus your energy.
- Values: Core values (what matters most to you?)
- Receivers: Who are you here to help?

Over the years I struggled to articulate my own mission statement, but eventually I arrived at one that I believe captures the essence of both my personal and professional life: "To encourage, affirm, and inspire meaningful connection, ongoing learning, and deeper growth both in myself and others as I invite fun, laughter, and play into my relationships."

A few key relationships have helped me persevere since I was a kid, so building secure, loving attachments has become a part of my life mission. If those sorts of quality relationships are still elusive for you, hold on to the possibility that there are emotionally reliable people out there.

Discovering Legacy

Let your future legacy be part of your life mission as well. Life is short and unpredictable, so from this point forward, consider what you would like to leave behind. It may be a material item or a character trait, and it can be big or small. Most of us don't think about our legacy because that requires thinking about death, and end-of-life issues are taboo in our society. But considering your and other people's legacies can be inspiring.

My grandmother lived a simple life, but the tremendous love she shared with my family lives on. Because our hearts were so closely intertwined, her legacy lives on in me. She wasn't a woman of strong financial means, but the way she donated her time and energy to others was bountiful. Nobody can ever replace her incomparable baking, and she fed me in so many other ways too that I am forever grateful. As I stated, my grandmother and my dog were the two primary reasons I survived my chaotic childhood. They are part of my Universal Energy.

How would you like to be remembered?

Colin: *As someone who mattered in people's lives. Did I make a difference in this world? Did I touch people in a way that affected them in a loving way? I hope so.*

Alex: *I want to be remembered as someone kind and gentle who didn't take himself too seriously. I want to say that I was someone who lived in my heart, not in my head.*

Seth: *That I'm a really good dad and partner.*

Mario: *As an agent of serenity, reassurance, and support.*

Robert: *As truthful and joyful, with a sense of humor and depth.*

As I ask myself this same question, it feels too big for words, but I hope my legacy is similar to my mission statement, though perhaps with a slight difference. My calling has been to help others be their best selves and experience love and deeper connection. But to put it another way, I believe my legacy is to give back what I've been given. Much love has been freely shared with me. So how would I like to be remembered? As a human who tried.

And like the Jewish scholar Hillel said, "If not now, when?"

Action Steps:

1. Don't be intimidated by spirituality. It's whatever gives your life meaning. Using this perspective, find what spirituality means to you.

2. Purpose includes love, kindness, beauty, and compassion. Be mindful of these elements in your everyday life. Track them for thirty days, and notice what happens inside of you.

3. A mission statement is a spiritual compass. If your actions and values align, you'll move forward with ease and flow. Write a mission statement that combines your values with actions and receivers.

4. One of recovery's most powerful gifts is the opportunity to give back to others. That generosity of spirit will be your legacy. Name a few recent occasions when you demonstrated other-centeredness most fully.

Chapter Twelve

It's Not the Mistakes That Count

Experience is simply the name we give our mistakes.
—Oscar Wilde

When you hear the word *forgiveness*, what's the first thing that comes to mind? Going to confession? Showing compassion to people who've wronged you? Or is it being apologized to? Whatever side of it you're on, forgiveness is among the most powerful, difficult, and transformative things you'll experience in life. It allows you to feel calmer, connected, and more whole.

In recovery, forgiveness strengthens your emotional sobriety. If you don't yet feel emotionally sober, you might consider what needs forgiving. For example, if you felt self-righteous about your decision to have an extramarital affair, believing that your partner deserved to be cheated on, and this attitude persists, there is more work to be done. If on the other hand you're willing to act differently in the future and be accountable for your part in all grudges, that's a sign of emotional sobriety, as you've taken responsibility for missteps in the past. Remember, it's not your mistakes that count. It's how you deal with them.

In twelve-step programs, the amends steps (eight and nine) target past actions. Showing up differently for yourself and others, now and from this point forward, takes a conscious decision to stay present and accountable in all relationships. That's how deeper connections grow. Making amends is not simply about apologizing—it's a daily effort to be kind and responsible and to clean up the wreckage of your past.

Forgiving Others

But how do you offer forgiveness in addition to asking for forgiveness? Most of all, how do you forgive yourself? Take a moment to reflect on the profound nature of personal and interpersonal forgiveness as you consider the following questions:

- What has forgiveness meant to you in the past?
- What does forgiveness mean to you today?
- How would you like to integrate forgiveness into your ongoing recovery?

Now take a moment to chart a *forgiveness map*—the ways forgiveness has been a part of your past, or not.

- Who have you chosen to forgive? Why?
- Who have you chosen not to forgive? Why?
- What may be unforgivable to you?
- Who has forgiven you for your past behaviors?

Forgiveness is often about timing. Check in with yourself as you consider these questions, to be sure you're ready for this step. If you're feeling openhearted to the process of forgiveness, continue on. If you're feeling unsure about it, take a break until you feel emotionally prepared to open this door. You'll know when it feels right to you. There's no specific way to participate in a forgiveness process. And remember that it is a process—not a one-time event. One myth about forgiveness is that it's solely about your past. Actually, it's about how you interpret past experiences through the lens of *today*. Only you will know if and when the time has arrived to forgive, and when it does, pace yourself, and invite a trusted confidant to be in your corner.

Making amends is like passing through a portal; on the other side of the forgiveness process is understanding and compassion for yourself and others. Keep in mind that love and blame cannot coexist. So the forgiveness process requires more love and less blame. Stepping away from your victimhood is a courageous choice. Leaning into love is an act of faith.

In my case, for many years I resented and blamed my mother for not being the type of parent I wanted. I longed for someone who would listen well and express interest in me, but this was not her forte. Unfortunately, for much of her life she was depressed and self-centered, which left me longing for more connection. Whether I lived with her or across the country, the disappointment inside of me festered. Then as I began to study psychology, I became even more condescending, frustrated, and self-righteous.

With lots of wise, loving guidance, I eventually learned to forgive and accept my mother for who she was. Thankfully, we had a chance to get closer after she was diagnosed with terminal cancer, and today I remember my mom with gratitude. I wouldn't be who I am today if not for her.

No matter how self-righteous you feel at the time, blaming and shaming isn't productive. If anything it exacerbates suffering, until you find a way to work through the charged feelings inside you. I highly encourage you to repair complicated relationships before it's too late. Even if you retain hurt feelings, you can have compassion for the people who caused them. Forgiveness and acceptance go hand in hand. Letting go of the bitterness will help relieve the pain, and vice versa; healing your pain will diminish lingering resentments. Ultimately you have a choice—hold on to the hurt, or process it and diminish its power.

This isn't to suggest that you forget about the past. That would be like losing a part of your identity. It's instead crucial that you come to terms with the past. As the wisdom of the Serenity Prayer states, "Grant me the serenity to *accept* the things I cannot change."

To forgive my mother, and myself for the ways I pushed her away, I needed to grieve the past and step fully into the tough reality of the present. By accepting our complicated emotional dynamic, I eventually developed more freedom and peace within our relationship. This opened up new understanding for other relationships and life experiences as well.

Due to the many layers of loss associated with out-of-control sexual behavior, it takes perseverance to accept the pain of your past on a daily basis. Healthy expressions of grief are what allow this forgiveness to occur. By saying goodbye to the fantasy mother I pined for in my imagination, I finally managed to value my real mother's efforts to have a relationship with me. Her humor, her dramatic flair, and her love of antiques stay with me today. I've learned to forgive her for her shortcomings as well as my own.

The gap between reality and "what could've been" is where disappointment and resentments are born. That disparity is also an opportunity to practice self-compassion. How you choose to interpret missed opportunities and process regret determines where your growth happens. Today you have the chance to move beyond the "shoulda, woulda, couldas," and move forward as you take purposeful action to achieve your recovery goals.

Sobriety cannot provide everything you want all of the time, but with the right point of view, you'll find that it offers exactly what you need. Your basic need to be understood, respected, and valued as a child wasn't always met. But in recovery you can lean into the love of dependable people and learn where and when support is available. As the twelve-step slogan goes, "Expectations are resentments under construction." It's okay to ask for specific things from others, knowing that you may not get exactly what you hoped for. Letting go of the results is a mature and liberating approach to life. As I've shared before, it's not that anything *has* to happen, but simply what *could* happen. This logic helps to prevent you from feeling locked into rigid standards for how your life should turn out.

Self-Forgiveness

After a slip or relapse, stay out of self-judgment to prevent yourself from falling into a shame spiral. Process it with a trusted confidant as soon as possible. Your setback happened for a reason. Were you trying to unwind some internal pressure? Express pent-up anger? Soothe yourself? Ask yourself what you were trying to accomplish. Can you find a better way to achieve it in the future? Explore these possibilities before you move on to self-forgiveness. By taking a closer look at your behavior, you'll prevent a spiritual bypass.

In my workbook *From Now On*, I suggest writing a self-forgiveness letter, and the instructions are as follows. Think about shame you experienced in the past that won't seem to go away. Cruel statements, infidelity, or financial losses from sex addiction, for example. Include:

1. A detailed description of what happened.
2. How this event haunts you.
3. How you choose to accept this experience as a part of your past and *not* a part of your present.
4. How you would like to say goodbye to it.
5. How to be more compassionate with yourself regarding this past behavior.

Writing a letter of self-forgiveness helps you grieve and accept yourself fully. You'll reduce the power resentment holds over you as you put these memories down on paper and reflect on how you'll move forward with an eye toward empathy. Practice loving kindness rather than complaining and blaming. Don't get caught in the trap of chronic commiseration. Consider these questions of self-compassion:

- In what ways are you willing to be more compassionate with yourself?
- How will you accept yourself unconditionally, warts and all?
- How do you forgive yourself?
- How do you hold back from forgiving yourself?

When applied as a daily practice, kindness creates new neural pathways to override the habit of self-criticism. Stop yourself each and every time you are unkind, to etch more loving instincts in your mind. As Dr. Donald Hebb said, "Neurons that fire together, wire together." If you complain on a consistent basis, that becomes your well-worn path.

One key feature of purposeful recovery is that you lean into healing practices such as self-acceptance, self-compassion, and self-forgiveness on a daily basis. Unfortunately many recovering sex addicts, both in the twelve-step rooms and elsewhere, continue to suffer by indulging in self-recrimination and pity. Complaining and misery can become their own compulsion. As long as you reinforce suffering with negative thoughts, recovery will be an uphill battle. But if you make the conscious choice to practice gratitude and forgiveness instead, you'll feel more emotionally sober. The practice of spiritual healing and loving kindness is a daily effort that requires discipline and patience.

Let me share the story of someone who dealt with mistakes and remorse in a positive, healthy way.

Case Study Twelve: Rick's Mistakes

Rick came from a lower-middle-class family outside of Chicago, and at the time, many men in the neighborhood went outside their marriages for sex. One day, Rick overheard his parents arguing and inadvertently learned that his father had been having several affairs, too. His mother put up with it, and Rick never let on that he knew. He suffered silently because he loved his parents, but also felt deeply ashamed of their arrangement.

In his twenties, Rick vowed to live his life differently, and gave himself strict rules for his own sexual behavior. He used porn moderately. At age thirty he married Alisa, and they had two kids rather quickly. Although Rick was in love with Alisa, he began to struggle with the pressures of marriage, fatherhood, and his career. He excelled in the IT field, but never thoroughly enjoyed it. While his life looked successful on the outside, by age forty Rick felt trapped.

To celebrate a major business deal, a colleague invited Rick out to a strip club, and the experience was intoxicating. He found this version of live porn far more satisfying than internet porn. It was like a switch flipped inside him as Rick fell into an unexpected, clandestine routine. He justified visits to strip clubs by telling himself it was isolated fun—not full-fledged affairs like his father's. But these secret experiences left Rick feeling ashamed and out of control.

When Alisa found the evidence of the porn and the strip clubs, she was devastated and asked Rick to get help. Though disillusioned and disgusted, she still loved him and wanted to mend their marriage. Rick went to his first twelve-step meeting and worked with a therapist who specialized in addiction and trauma. From the beginning, Rick recognized his sexual compulsion as a problem based in his childhood heartbreak. For twelve years he immersed himself in working the steps, being a sponsor to others, and attending a weekly men's therapy group.

Then at age fifty-two, Rick did something that took him, his wife, his therapist, and his sponsor all by surprise. He had run into his favorite stripper at a supermarket, and afterward started visiting her again at the club. He'd been keeping this secret. He even fantasized that he could escape his current life and start a family with her.

"I don't think words can describe how ashamed I feel," Rick says. "But I don't want to make excuses for my behavior. The fantasy makes no rational sense. I've just been feeling suffocated in my life. All I know is that I was becoming complacent and disconnected from myself and those I love."

Rick had been seen as a pillar in his fellowship.

"I'm a regular at my home meeting of SA (Sexaholics Anonymous). People look up to me there. After my wife found my porn stash and the emails I sent to strippers, I hit bottom and crawled to my first meeting. I remember an old-timer telling me that all I had to do was 'suit up and show up,' so I did. It's been twelve years since I found SA, and once again I feel like a newcomer there."

It's not the mistakes that matter; it's how you deal with them. Rick truly was remorseful, and he received clear direction from his therapist and sponsor to end the emotional affair and re-visit his challenges with vulnerability, trust, and intimacy in a more intensive way. He began to understand his ingrained style of love avoidance, and came clean with his twelve-step comrades and fellow group members.

Alisa and Rick found a talented couples therapist who helped them have honest conversations, with an emphasis on what had gone unexpressed in their marriage. They did not want to divorce, and Rick did not want to replicate his parents' fate. As painful as it was for both of them, the relationship with the stripper became a catalyst for a marriage makeover. Alisa started seeing a therapist too, and joined a women's support group to create a parallel healing path.

Mending their broken hearts felt slow, but over time, both Rick and Alisa felt more hopeful and close to one another. Their shared values, love, and family provided a strong foundation for the desire to move forward. As a result, mutual trust, respect, and understanding will continue to grow, along with their consistent commitment to learn about themselves and each other.

Residual Shame

There is a shame epidemic in the twelve-step community that leaves people at higher risk of relapse and suffering. I'm sure many of you are your own toughest critic. But if you took a poll of your most trustworthy dolphins, you would find that you are loved despite your mistakes. Isn't it time you tame your inner critic once and for all? Hopefully, over the course of this book you've turned the shame volume down. It may return and crescendo, however, when you have a slip or relapse.

When you criticize yourself or go on a "self-attack," take note of it. Why are you being so critical? Do you notice when you're doing this to yourself? What purpose does it serve? Self-attacks wall you off from others. It's an inferior position that keeps you in shame. Be curious and pay attention to any patterns you find. Rather than being one-up or one-down, consider right-sizing, because that's where true connection and intimacy exists.

Self-judgment brings you down, especially at times of relapse or slips. When you've broken a bottom-line behavior, indicating a slip, treat it as an opportunity to seek help from a sponsor or confidant to fine-tune your sexual recovery plan. If you're not in a program, ask a therapist or coach to help. Be aware that your definition of sexual sobriety will evolve over time. Unlike alcoholism, where you "put a plug in the jug," there are more nuances and gray areas with process addictions. Complete abstinence is neither desirable nor realistic, and even boundaries will be flexible over time.

You're Not Alone

In my therapy office, clients reveal setbacks all the time, and together we process their so-called mistakes. So what do you do if you've been in recovery for a while and then go off your plan? The tendency may be to isolate and keep it a secret, but this will only perpetuate the shame that goes along with the slip-up. Instead, contact someone you trust as soon as possible—preferably someone in recovery. They will offer their version of *experience, strength, and hope* with you. Immediately you'll realize you don't have to go through it alone. After you get current with someone who has walked in your shoes, talk about it at a meeting, or with your therapist or coach. Be as transparent as possible. Every mistake begins a new chapter in your discovery process. Journal, work your steps, lean into your healing team, and take direction from those who have been there.

Breaking your bottom-line behaviors is not a measure of who you are; it's a sign that it's time to establish healthier, more effective sexual boundaries. When you have a slip, remember that relapse is a part of recovery from sexual compulsivity. And it's not the relapse that matters so much as how you identify it, how quickly you ask for help, and how you get to know the shadow part of yourself better. Never measure your worth as a person by the amount of time you have away from your bottom-lines. Measure your worth by your willingness to pursue a healing path on a daily basis and sustain meaningful connection. Remember, recovery is about *progress, not perfection.*

Many years ago, I worked with a group of terrific hospice nurses who were also talented wound care nurses, and this is what I learned. Wounds require lots of attention. The bandages and dressing need to be changed several times a day to keep the wounds clean. They also require oxygen to properly heal. If you cover a wound with a sealed Band-Aid, it festers. So healing takes patience, consistency, air, and a touch of love. Emotional wounds—or slips—require these same elements to mend.

Don't just cover them up. Get familiar with your wounds and treat them diligently. It takes a healing team to mend your broken heart.

Riding the waves of regret is part of the deal, but when regrets turn into a way of life, they no longer serve a purpose. Stay out of a self-punitive, victim mode as you surround yourself with kind, loving energy. Get a reality check from the wisest people you know, and whatever you do, don't hibernate. Stay connected to others.

Consider the following analogy. If you're driving from New York to Los Angeles and you get a flat tire in Des Moines, does this mean you have to go back to New York? Of course not. You get the tire fixed and keep driving. It's the same way with sexual compulsivity. If you have a slip or a full-blown relapse, you have choices. Do you punish yourself, keep it a secret, and go into shame over it? Or do you learn from it and move forward?

I used to be a master at self-punishment when I made a mistake. Nowadays, I try to see my setbacks as growth opportunities. I examine parts of myself that need more attention, understanding, and acceptance. Although I can still fall into shame spirals once in a while, the time it takes for me to reconnect with my support network afterward has become more rapid, allowing me to mobilize rather than get stuck.

After a relapse, you can fall into shame and judgment, or you can learn from your error and move on. Don't be a victim. Hold yourself accountable to learn the lessons the mistake provides, and practice self-compassion. Recovery is not a linear progression. It's imperfect and unpredictable. You may stumble and fumble and go off course at times. But most of all, stay connected, lean into the love, and know that if you hang in there it will get better.

Acknowledgments

At its core, this book is about giving and receiving love, and I want to express my deepest gratitude to those who freely shared their love with me through the years:

My effusively loving grandmother Rose, my inspiring Aunt Ruth, my canine teachers Nikki, Cooper, and Bowie, my mentors Jesse, Sam, Burt, Cindy, and Jody. My loyal assistant Mike, and my gifted consultant Jean-Noel. My parents, my East and West Coast families of choice, and my kind, loving husband Mariano.

Six honest and emotionally generous individuals who volunteered to be interviewed for this book. Their stories represent a sliver of the brokenheartedness and courage shared with me over the past quarter of a century, both in my office and in the twelve-step rooms.

Most of all, I am grateful to Central Recovery Press for believing in this passion project. To Eliza Tutellier, who first opened the door to this collaboration with the CRP team. And a heartfelt thanks to Dan Hernandez, Senior Editor, a master gardener who pulled out all the weeds and designed a cohesive landscape.

Resources

Twelve-Step Programs for Sexual Addiction and Compulsivity

Sex Addicts Anonymous (SAA)
(800) 477-8191
saa-recovery.org

Sex and Love Addicts Anonymous (SLAA)
(210) 828-7900
www.slaafws.org

Sexaholics Anonymous (SA)
(615) 370-6062
www.sa.org

Sexual Compulsives Anonymous (SCA)
(800) 977-HEAL
sca-recovery.org

Twelve-Step Programs for Significant Others, Loved Ones, & Couples

COSA
(866) 899-2672
www.cosa-recovery.org

Recovering Couples Anonymous (RCA)
(877) 663-2317
recovering-couples.org

S-Anon International Family Groups
(800) 210-8141
www.sanon.org

Trauma Healing Practices

Brainspotting
brainspotting.com
www.brainspottinglosangeles.org

Sensorimotor Psychotherapy
www.sensorimotorpsychotherapy.org

Eye Movement Desensitization and
Reprocessing (EMDR)
www.emdr.com

Somatic Experiencing Trauma Institute (SE)
traumahealing.org

NeuroAffective Relational Model (NARM)   Trauma Resource Institute (TRM)
www.drlaurenceheller.com   www.traumaresourceinstitute.com

Additional Resources

American Association of Sexuality Educators, Counselors and Therapists (AASECT)
www.aasect.org

American Group Psychotherapy Association (AGPA)
www.agpa.org

International Coach Federation (ICF)
coachfederation.org

International Institute for Trauma and Addiction Professionals (IITAP)
iitap.com

Society for the Advancement of Sexual Health (SASH)
www.sash.net

Bibliography

American Psychiatric Association. *Diagnostic and Statistical Manual of Mental Disorders: DSM-5*. 5th ed. Washington, DC: American Psychiatric Publishing, 2013.

Bauer, Jan. *Impossible Love: Or Why the Heart Must Go Wrong*. Woodstock, CT: Spring Publications, 1993.

Beattie, Melody. *Codependent No More: How to Stop Controlling Others and Start Caring for Yourself*. Center City, MN: Hazelden, 1986.

Bowlby, John. *A Secure Base: Parent-Child Attachment and Healthy Human Development*. London: Routledge, 1988.

Bradshaw, John. *Healing the Shame that Binds You*, rev. ed. Deerfield Beach, FL: HCI, 2005.

Brown, Brené. *The Gifts of Imperfection: Let Go of Who You Think You're Supposed to Be and Embrace Who You Are*. Center City, MN: Hazelden, 2010.

Campbell, Chellie. *The Wealthy Spirit: Daily Affirmations for Financial Stress Reduction*. Naperville, IL: Sourcebooks, 2002.

Canfield, Jack. *The Success Principles: How to Get from Where You Are to Where You Want to Be*. New York: Harper Collins, 2005.

Carnes, Patrick. *Facing the Shadow: Starting Sexual and Relationship Recovery*. 3rd ed. Carefree, AZ: Gentle Path Press, 2015.

Dayton, Tian. *Emotional Sobriety: From Relationship Trauma to Resilience and Balance*. Deerfield Beach, FL: HCI, 2007.

Flores, Philip J. *Addiction as an Attachment Disorder*. New York: Jason Aronson, 2004.

Glass, Rawland. "*Codependency: The Elusive 'Ism.'*" Lecture, Los Angeles, CA, 2011.

Grand, David. *Brainspotting: The Revolutionary New Therapy for Rapid and Effective Change*. Louisville, CO: Sounds True, 2013.

Hebb, Donald O. *The Organization of Behavior: A Neuropsychological Theory*. Hoboken, NJ: John Wiley and Sons, 1949.

Kabat-Zinn, Jon. *Full Catastrophe Living: Using the Wisdom of Your Body and Mind to Face Stress, Pain, and Illness*, rev. ed. New York: Bantam, 2013.

Kain, Kathy L. "Somatic Experiencing" Presentation, Burlingame, CA, 2009.

Kellogg, Terry. *Broken Toys Broken Dreams: Understanding and Healing Codependency, Compulsive Behaviors and Family Relationships*. Amherst, MA: BRAT Publishing, 1990.

Kübler-Ross, Elisabeth. *On Death and Dying: What the Dying Have to Teach Doctors, Nurses, Clergy and Their Own Families*. New York: Scribner, 1993.

Levine, Peter. *Waking the Tiger: Healing Trauma*. Berkeley, CA: North Atlantic Books, 1997.

Lyubomirsky, Sonja. *The How of Happiness: A New Approach to Getting the Life You Want*, rev. ed. New York: Penguin, 2008.

Mellody, Pia. *Facing Love Addiction: Giving Yourself the Power to Change the Way You Love*. San Francisco, CA: Harper One, 2003.

"*Post-Induction Therapy.*" Training Presentation. Scottsdale, AZ, 2010.

Miller, James E. *A Pilgrimage Through Grief: Healing the Soul's Hurt After Loss*. Fort Wayne, IN: Willowgreen, 1995.

Miller-Karas, Elaine. *Building Resilience to Trauma: The Trauma and Community Resiliency Models*. New York: Routledge, 2015.

Nelson, Portia. *There's a Hole in My Sidewalk: The Romance of Self-Discovery*, rev. ed. New York: Atria Books, 2012.

Perel, Esther. *Mating in Captivity: Unlocking Erotic Intelligence*. 2006. Reprint, New York: Harper, 2017.

Rogers, Carl R. *On Becoming a Person: A Therapist's View of Psychotherapy.* Boston: Houghton Mifflin, 1961.

Rothschild, Babette. *The Body Remembers: The Psychophysiology of Trauma and Trauma Treatment.* New York: Norton, 2000.

Seligman, Martin. *Flourish: A Visionary New Understanding of Happiness and Well-being.* 2011. Reprint, New York: Atria Books, 2012.

Selye, Hans. *The Stress of Life.* 2nd ed. New York: McGraw-Hill, 1978.

Sex and Love Addicts Anonymous: *The Basic Text for the Augustine Fellowship Sex and Love Addicts Anonymous,* Augustine Fellowship, 1986.

Siegel, Daniel J. *The Developing Mind: How Relationships and the Brain Interact to Shape Who We Are.* 2nd ed. *New York: Guilford Press,* 2012.

Skinner, B.F. *Science and Human Behavior,* New Impression ed. New York: The Free Press, 1965.

World Health Organization. *International Statistical Classification of Diseases and Related Health Problems, 10th edition, ICD-11.* Washington, DC: American Psychiatric Publishing, 1992.